THE
CULTIC PROPHET IN ANCIENT ISRAEL

By

AUBREY R. JOHNSON

CARDIFF
UNIVERSITY OF WALES PRESS
1962

FIRST EDITION 1944
SECOND EDITION 1962

PRINTED IN GREAT BRITAIN

045556

TO THE MEMORY OF
MY PARENTS
FRANK JOHNSON
BEATRICE MARY JOHNSON

PREFACE

IN preparing the revised edition of this monograph I have
not attempted to refer in detail to the growing number of
those students of the Old Testament who accept in principle
the theory of cultic prophets; nor have I thought it necessary to answer or even cite those critics of the theory who
(i) begin with some preconceived notion as to what con-
stitutes a 'prophet', or (ii) attribute to me, quite unwarrantably, the view that all the canonical prophets were cultic
prophets. Indeed, with regard to the latter point I must
evidently beg some of my readers to note that, apart from
a passing comment which could hardly be avoided, I make
no attempt in this monograph to deal with the complicated
question as to whether or not any of the canonical prophets
are to be regarded as cultic prophets. The fact is that we
are not yet at the stage where this question can be discussed
in anything like a satisfactory way. The whole subject of
prophecy in ancient Israel is much more complex than is
commonly recognized; and in this revised edition of my
work I have felt it necessary to draw attention more than
once to the disservice to Old Testament study which may be
done by over-simplifying the issues and resorting to easy
generalizations. It is my earnest hope that the following
pages will serve to bring out something of the complexity
of these issues and, at the same time, make some small
contribution towards the solution of a few of the associated
problems. In this connexion perhaps I should seek to avoid
further inquiry by adding that I have now completed the
greater part of the promised sequel to this monograph which
was to appear under the title *The Cultic Prophet and the
Psalter* (cf. first edition, p. 5, n. 1), and that I hope to see it
through the press as soon as I have met the need to issue
revised editions of the other monographs in this series.

It now remains for me to acknowledge my indebtedness

to the many colleagues and friends who have helped me in the preparation of this work, particularly Professor Otto Eissfeldt, who first drew my attention to the theory of cultic prophets as long ago as my postgraduate days in Halle, and encouraged me to look into the question on the ground that it might have some bearing on what seemed to me to be the role of the king in the Jerusalem cultus; my revered teacher, Professor Theodore H. Robinson, who, if he viewed some of my conclusions with certain misgivings, showed characteristic generosity in giving me unfailing encouragement to go my own way; Professor N. W. Porteous and Professor H. H. Rowley for their constant interest and encouragement, tempered now and again with constructive criticism of an invaluable kind; Professor A. Jirku and Dr. P. Wernberg-Møller for the loan of books which I was finding it difficult to consult; and, once again, the Reverend C. G. Williams for his ready help with the reading of the proofs and the preparation of the indexes.

I must also repeat here the acknowledgement due to the editors of *The Expository Times* for their kind permission to draw freely upon the text of my article, 'The Prophet in Israelite Worship' (vol. xlvii (1935–6), pp. 312–19: cf. first edition, p. 5, n. 1); and, finally, it is a pleasure to renew my warm thanks to the University of Wales Press for accepting my monographs for publication and to the Oxford University Press for the patience and skill with which they are produced.

AUBREY R. JOHNSON

Cardiff
July 1961

PRINCIPAL ABBREVIATIONS

A.J.S.L.	*American Journal of Semitic Languages and Literatures.*
A.T.A.N.T.	Abhandlungen zur Theologie des Alten und Neuen Testaments.
A.T.D.	Das Alte Testament Deutsch.
B.A.	*The Biblical Archaeologist.*
B.A.E.R.(W.)	*Bureau of American Ethnology Reports (Washington).*
B.D.B.	Brown, Driver, and Briggs, *A Hebrew and English Lexicon of the Old Testament* (1906), corrected impression (1952).
B.F.C.T.	Beiträge zur Förderung christlicher Theologie.
B.J.R.L.	*Bulletin of the John Rylands Library.*
B.O.T.	De Boeken van het Oude Testament.
B.Q.	*The Baptist Quarterly.*
B.W.A.N.T.	Beiträge zur Wissenschaft vom Alten und Neuen Testament.
B.W.A.T.	Beiträge zur Wissenschaft vom Alten Testament.
B.Z.A.W.	Beihefte zur *Zeitschrift für die alttestamentliche Wissenschaft.*
C.B.	Cambridge Bible.
Cent.B.	The Century Bible.
D	The Deuteronomic narrative (*or* code), or the Deuteronomic school.
D.B.	*A Dictionary of the Bible*, ed. J. Hastings (1898–1904).
E	The Elohistic narrative (*or* code), or the Elohist.
E.B.	Études Bibliques.
E.B.	*Encyclopaedia Biblica*, ed. T. K. Cheyne and J. S. Black (1899–1903).
Echt.B.	Echter Bibel.
E.H.P.R.	Études d'histoire et de philosophie religieuses.
E.R.E.	*The Encyclopaedia of Religion and Ethics*, ed. J. Hastings (1908–26).
E.T.	*The Expository Times.*
G.T.M.M.M.	Det Gamle Testamente, oversatt av S. Michelet, S. Mowinckel og N. Messel.
H.A.T.	Handbuch zum Alten Testament.
H.K.	Handkommentar zum Alten Testament.
H.S.A.T.	Die Heilige Schrift des Alten Testamentes (Bonner Bibel).
H.S.A.T.	E. Kautzsch (ed.), *Die Heilige Schrift des Alten Testaments*, 4th edition, ed. A. Bertholet (1922–3).
H.U.C.A.	*Hebrew Union College Annual.*
I.B.	The Interpreter's Bible.
I.C.C.	The International Critical Commentary.
J	The Yahwistic narrative (*or* code), or the Yahwist.

J.A.I.	*Journal of the Anthropological Institute.*
J.B.L.	*Journal of Biblical Literature.*
J.P.	*The Journal of Philology.*
J.P.O.S.	*The Journal of the Palestine Oriental Society.*
J.Q.R.	*Jewish Quarterly Review.*
J.T.S.	*The Journal of Theological Studies.*
K.A.T.	Kommentar zum Alten Testament.
K.B.	L. Koehler and W. Baumgartner, *Lexicon in Veteris Testamenti Libros* (1953), including *Supplementum ad Lexicon in Veteris Testamenti Libros* (1958).
K.H.C.	Kurzer Hand-Commentar zum Alten Testament.
K.K.	Kurzgefasster Kommentar zu den heiligen Schriften Alten und Neuen Testamentes sowie zu den Apokryphen.
LXX	The Septuagint.
Nor.T.T.	*Norsk Teologisk Tidsskrift.*
N.T.T.	*Nieuw Theologisch Tijdschrift.*
O.T.S.	Old Testament Studies.
O.T.S.	*Oudtestamentische Studiën.*
P	The Priestly narrative (*or* code), or the Priestly school.
P.W.K.	Pauly–Wissowa–Kroll, *Real-Encyclopädie der classischen Altertumswissenschaft* (1894–).
R.G.G.	*Die Religion in Geschichte und Gegenwart*, 1st edition, ed. F. M. Schiele and L. Zscharnack (1909–13), 2nd edition, ed. H. Gunkel and L. Zscharnack (1927–32), 3rd edition, ed. K. Galling (1957–).
R.H.P.R.	*Revue d'histoire et de philosophie religieuses.*
R.H.R.	*Revue de l'histoire des religions.*
S	The Syriac Version (Peshiṭta).
S.A.T.	Die Schriften des Alten Testaments in Auswahl.
S.B.J.	La Sainte Bible traduite en français sous la direction de l'École Biblique de Jérusalem.
S.B.U.	Symbolae Biblicae Upsalienses.
S.N.V.A.O. II.	Skrifter utgitt av Det Norske Videnskaps-Akademi i Oslo, II. Hist.-Filos. Klasse.
S.O.E.D.	*The Shorter Oxford English Dictionary.*
S.V.T.	Supplements to *Vetus Testamentum.*
T	Targum.
Th.W.N.T.	*Theologisches Wörterbuch zum Neuen Testament*, ed. G. Kittel and G. Friedrich (1933–).
T.T.	*Theologisch Tijdschrift.*
T.U.	Tekst en Uitleg.
T.Z.	*Theologische Zeitschrift.*
V.T.	*Vetus Testamentum.*
W.C.	Westminster Commentaries.
Z.A.W.	*Zeitschrift für die alttestamentliche Wissenschaft.*
Z.D.M.G.	*Zeitschrift der deutschen morgenländischen Gesellschaft.*

THE CULTIC PROPHET IN ANCIENT ISRAEL

I

A T first sight the Old Testament seems to furnish a straightforward account of the history of Israel from its earliest times until the latter part of the fifth century B.C. The critical study of the Old Testament, however, has shown that this semblance of unity is probably due to the efforts of various centres or schools of thought which found literary expression between the tenth and the fourth centuries B.C.[1]

[1] Cf., for example, J. Hempel, *Die althebräische Literatur und ihr hellenistisch-jüdisches Nachleben* (1930–4); O. Eissfeldt, *Einleitung in das Alte Testament* (1934), 2nd edit. rev. (1956); W. O. E. Oesterley and T. H. Robinson, *An Introduction to the Books of the Old Testament* (1934); A. Weiser, *Einleitung in das Alte Testament* (1939), 4th edit. rev. (1957); R. H. Pfeiffer, *Introduction to the Old Testament* (1941); A. Bentzen, *Introduction to the Old Testament* (1946), 2nd edit. rev. (1952); G. W. Anderson, *A Critical Introduction to the Old Testament* (1959). An outstanding feature of the works by Hempel, Eissfeldt, Weiser, Bentzen, and Anderson is the marked attention given to 'form criticism' (*Formgeschichte*) with its concern for the 'setting in life' (*Sitz im Leben*) of the various literary 'types' (*Gattungen*) which have gone to the making of the Old Testament. The influence of this approach in so far as it affects the Psalter will be recognizable by the reader in the immediate sequel to this monograph, just as it may also be observed in the writer's companion study *Sacral Kingship in Ancient Israel* (1955). Further, despite recent attempts to lay greater stress on the part played in the development of Israel's historical records by oral tradition and the forms of worship at the different sanctuaries, there remain ample grounds for the acceptance in principle of what is commonly known as the Graf–Kuenen–Wellhausen critical reconstruction of the origin and growth of the historical books of the Old Testament. Cf., in addition to the foregoing works by Eissfeldt, Weiser, Bentzen, and Anderson, the balanced survey of recent Pentateuchal criticism which is given by C. R. North in *The Old Testament and Modern Study*, ed. H. H. Rowley (1951), pp. 48–83. Greater reserve is necessary, however, with regard to the general attempt to present the religion of Israel in its historical development which is characteristic of the so-called Wellhausen school. Early doubts on the part of the writer as to the trustworthiness of this almost too clear a picture of the course of events (involving what appeared to be an over-emphasis upon the role assigned to the canonical prophets in this scheme) soon found confirmation of an acceptable kind through the instructive article by J. Pedersen, 'Die Auffassung vom Alten Testament', *Z.A.W.* xlix (1931), pp. 161–81; and, somewhat later, these doubts found equally

In the nature of the case this statement does not apply so much to the supposed records from, say, the ninth and eighth centuries B.C. which are represented by the so-called 'Yahwistic' (J) and 'Elohistic' (E) elements in the Old Testament. It applies rather to those later schools of thought which are represented by the so-called 'Deuteronomic' (D) and 'Priestly' (P) records. Of these the former is generally thought to have come into existence during the seventh century, and it is this school which most strikingly introduces the semblance of unity. It does so by a process of editing such previous records as cover the period from the time of the settlement in Canaan until the fall of Jerusalem (587 B.C.) and the Babylonian Exile (587–538 B.C.). The P school, which seems to have flourished in the fifth century, completes the semblance of unity, and it succeeds in this by means of another editorial process which deals with the whole period of Israelite history from the earliest times down to the first part of the fourth century. Further, these two schools reveal, not only the gradual claim to a monopoly of worship on behalf of the Jerusalem Temple and its personnel, but also the growing influence of a cultic specialist—namely the כֹּהֵן or 'priest'. The following pages are intended to show that, both in general and particularly as regards the Jerusalem Temple, the נָבִיא or 'prophet' originally filled a cultic role of at least equal, if not greater, importance.[1]

acceptable reinforcement in the similar strictures upon the misleading influence of Hegelian philosophy and somewhat too facile theories of 'evolution' made by W. F. Albright, 'The Ancient Near East and the Religion of Israel', *J.B.L.* lix (1940), pp. 91 ff.; *From the Stone Age to Christianity* (1940), 2nd edit. rev. (1946), with a new introduction (1957), chap. ii. Tribute should also be paid to the stimulating work by J. H. Breasted, *The Dawn of Conscience* (1934).

[1] It need hardly be said that students of the Old Testament have often recognized that at least the early type of נָבִיא (and, not infrequently, the later type combated, for example, by Jeremiah) was connected in some way with the sanctuary and its attendant priesthood. W. R. Smith, for example, speaks of such נְבִיאִים as 'living together in the neighbourhood of ancient sanctuaries . . . and in all likelihood closely connected with the priests, as was certainly the case in Judah down to the extinction of the state (Jer. xxix. 26, cf. xx. 1, 2; Lam. ii. 20, &c.). The prophets of Jehovah and the priests of

By way of providing further background to this study we may bear in mind the fact that in the earliest records the לֵוִי or 'Levite', as a cultic official, always has the status of a כֹּהֵן or 'priest'.[1] This is also true of D, where it holds good of

Jehovah were presumably associated much as were the prophets and priests of Baal.'—*The Prophets of Israel*, 2nd edit. with additional notes by T. K. Cheyne (1895), p. 85. It is only in recent years, however, that the possible extent of this association has been recognized; and this has been brought about through focusing attention upon the possibility that among the literary types (*Gattungen*) discernible in the Old Testament, notably the oracular elements in the Psalter (to say nothing, at this stage, about the books of the canonical prophets), we actually have traces of the work of such cultic נְבִיאִים. The pioneer treatise in this field was that of S. Mowinckel, *Psalmenstudien III: Kultprophetie und prophetische Psalmen*, S.N.V.A.O. II, 1922, No. 1 (1923); see also *Le Décalogue*, E.H.P.R. 16 (1927), pp. 125 ff. After the appearance of the former work, however, this theory was advocated in different ways by several continental scholars, notably A. Causse, *Les Plus Vieux Chants de la Bible*, E.H.P.R. 14 (1926), pp. 125 ff.; H. Junker, *Prophet und Seher in Israel* (1927), *passim*; Hempel, op. cit., pp. 33 ff., 56 ff.; Eissfeldt, op. cit., pp. 75 ff., 116 ff. (2nd edit., pp. 80 ff., 121 ff.). See also, with more general reference to such cultic prophets, W. Eichrodt, *Theologie des Alten Testaments*, i (1933), pp. 162–78 (5th edit. rev. (1957), pp. 204–25); G. von Rad, 'Die falschen Propheten', *Z.A.W.* li (1933), pp. 109–20; J. Pedersen, *Israel III–IV: Hellighed og Guddommelighed* (1934), pp. 84 ff. (E.T. *Israel: its Life and Culture III–IV* (1940), 2nd edit. with additions (1959), pp. 107 ff.): and cf. A. Jepsen, *Nabi: Soziologische Studien zur alttestamentlichen Literatur und Religionsgeschichte* (1934), pp. 154 ff., 191 ff. For a careful appraisal of the whole theory in all its issues in so far as these have been developed and discussed since the drawing up of the foregoing list of references for the first edition of this work, see H. H. Rowley, 'The Nature of Old Testament Prophecy in the Light of Recent Study', in *The Servant of the Lord and Other Essays on the Old Testament* (1952), pp. 89–128; and 'Ritual and the Hebrew Prophets', in *Myth, Ritual, and Kingship*, ed. S. H. Hooke (1958), pp. 236–60. The examination of the problem which is reproduced in these pages and has yet to be developed in connexion with the Psalter is intended (*a*) as a supplement to the writer's study of the cultic role of the king as originally formulated in *The Labyrinth: Further Studies in the Relation between Myth and Ritual in the Ancient World*, ed. S. H. Hooke (1935), pp. 71–111, and as finally elaborated in *Sacral Kingship in Ancient Israel* (see the previous note and the preface to the work cited); and (*b*) as an aid to a better understanding of the canonical prophets *vis-à-vis* the cultic forms of Israel's religious life. In connexion with the latter point, however, it may be as well to reiterate here what has already been said in the preface to this edition, i.e. that, apart from an occasional comment which could hardly be avoided, the writer makes no attempt at this stage to deal with the further question as to whether or not any of the canonical prophets are to be regarded as cultic prophets.

[1] Cf., for example, G. B. Gray, *Sacrifice in the Old Testament* (1925), pp. 211 ff., 239 ff.

any Levite whether belonging to the immediate personnel of the Jerusalem Temple or (as formerly attached to one of the local sanctuaries) holding office in the outlying districts; and, theoretically at least, those in the latter case have an equal right with those in the former to serve at Yahweh's altar in Jerusalem.[1] On the other hand, in Ezekiel xl–xlviii (a piece of exilic legislation dealing with the Jerusalem cultus)[2] such service at Yahweh's altar, which is here represented as a specifically 'priestly' function,[3] is restricted amongst other things to the Levitical house of Zadok; and all remaining Levites are reduced to a subordinate position.[4] Somewhat similarly the P school restricts the priesthood proper to the Levitical house of Aaron, and thus draws a distinction between the Aaronite כֹּהֵן or 'priest', who again has the prerogative of service at Yahweh's altar in the Temple at Jerusalem,[5] and the ordinary לֵוִי or 'Levite', who is a subordinate cultic official—for example, a 'porter' or (rather more significantly in the present connexion) a member of one of the so-called 'choirs'.[6]

Further, whether or not one may call to aid the etymology of the terms כֹּהֵן[7] and לֵוִי,[8] there can be no doubt that origin-

---

[1] Gray, op. cit., pp. 226 ff.

[2] Cf., for example, Eissfeldt, op. cit., 2nd edit., pp. 453–65.

[3] xliv. 9 ff.: see below, p. 8.   [4] Gray, loc. cit.

[5] Cf. Exod. xxviii ff.; Lev. i ff.: and see below, p. 8.

[6] Gray, op. cit., pp. 228 ff. Cf., too, with regard to the last point, W. R. Smith, *The Old Testament in the Jewish Church*, 2nd edit. rev. (1892), pp. 203 ff.; and see below, pp. 69 ff.

[7] Cf. Gray's full discussion of the use of this term and its cognates (particularly the Arabic كَاهِن, 'seer' or 'diviner'), op. cit., pp. 181 ff.: and, for the etymology, see also E. (P.) Dhorme, 'Prêtres, devins et mages dans l'ancienne religion des Hébreux', *R.H.R.* cviii (1933), pp. 117 f., *L'Évolution religieuse d'Israël. I: La Religion des Hébreux nomades* (1937), p. 225; R. de Vaux, *Les Institutions de l'Ancien Testament*, ii (1960), p. 196. As for Gray's inclination to accept the view that the Arabic كَاهِن is really a loan-word and his claim that the term under discussion 'is most naturally attributed to Canaan rather than to a pre-Canaanite stage of the history of the Hebrews' (op. cit., p. 183), it should be observed that in the Ugaritic texts of the fourteenth century B.C., which have come to light since Gray's work was published, the corresponding term occurs several times in the plural, notably

ally the principal function of the cultic officials denoted by both was the giving of oracular direction.[1] Thus in the so-called 'Blessing of Moses',[2] a composite work which is usually assigned in its present form to the latter part of the tenth or the early part of the eighth century B.C.,[3] the Levites are characterized as follows:[4]

(Give unto Levi)[5] Thy Tummim,
    And Thine Urim to him who is pledged to Thee,[6]
Whom Thou didst put on trial at Massah (i.e. 'Trial'),
    With whom Thou didst contend by the waters of Meribah (i.e.
    'Contention');
Who saith of his father and mother, 'I see them not',
    Nor doth he recognize his brothers or know his children.
For they guard Thy dictates,[7]

in the expression *rb khnm*, 'chief of the priests'. Cf., for example, C. H. Gordon, *Ugaritic Manual* (1955), ii. 62, 54 f. = G. R. Driver, *Canaanite Myths and Legends*, O.T.S. 3 (1956), B I vi. 18. For the actual figure of the كَاهِن, see J. Pedersen, 'The Rôle played by Inspired Persons among the Israelites and the Arabs', in *Studies in Old Testament Prophecy* (T. H. Robinson *Festschrift*), ed. H. H. Rowley (1950), pp. 133 ff.

[8] Cf. the summary of the position to date which is given by G. Hölscher, P.W.K. xxiv Halbband (1925), art. 'Levi': and see now, in supplementation of Gray, op. cit., pp. 242 ff., W. F. Albright, *Archaeology and the Religion of Israel*, 3rd edit. rev. (1953), pp. 109, 204 f., and, in the German translation by F. Cornelius (with additions by the author), *Die Religion Israels im Lichte der archäologischen Ausgrabungen* (1956), pp. 124 f., 228; de Vaux, op. cit., pp. 213 f., 228 f.; G. Fohrer, *R.G.G.*[3] iv (1960), art. 'Levi und Leviten'.

[1] Cf., in addition to the works cited below, Gray, op. cit., pp. 219 ff.; also, with special reference to the priestly oracle as a literary type, Hempel, op. cit., pp. 69 ff., and (with fuller references to the relevant literature) Eissfeldt, op. cit., pp. 80 ff.   [2] Deut. xxxiii.

[3] Cf., for example, G. A. Smith, *Deuteronomy*, C.B. (1918), pp. 360 ff., and (again with fuller references to the relevant literature) Eissfeldt, op. cit., pp. 271 ff.   [4] Verses 8 ff.   [5] So LXX.

[6] *lit.* 'Thy devoted one' or 'Thy votary', 'Thy devotee'. For חֶסֶד (EVV. 'mercy', 'kindness', 'lovingkindness') as having the basic implication of 'devotion' and חָסִיד (EVV. 'saint', 'holy', 'godly', 'merciful', &c.) as meaning one who is 'devoted', i.e. a 'votary' or 'devotee' or even in certain contexts one who is 'devout', see the writer's discussion of the use of these terms in *Interpretationes ad Vetus Testamentum pertinentes* (S. Mowinckel *Festschrift*) = *Nor.T.T.* lvi, 1–2 Hefte (1955), pp. 100–12.

[7] For the force of אִמְרָה in this connexion, cf. the use of the cognate root in Arabic, e.g. أَمَرَ, 'to command'.

And keep watch over Thy covenant;
They give direction to Jacob in Thy מִשְׁפָּטִים,
And to Israel in Thy תּוֹרָה;
They set the smoke of sacrifice in Thy Nostrils,
And holocausts upon Thine altar.

Here the service at Yahweh's altar is obviously subsidiary; the primary function of the Levite is to give direction[1] in the matter of Yahweh's commands. As means to this end he possesses two channels of knowledge. The first of these is indicated by the reference to the Urim (אוּרִים) and Tummim (תֻּמִּים), and is that of the sacred lot with its simple provision for an affirmative or negative response.[2] The second is made clear by the reference to his laying down

---

[1] For a full, if somewhat controversial, study of the forms הוֹרָה, 'to direct, teach', and תּוֹרָה, 'direction, teaching, law', see G. Östborn, *Tōrā in the Old Testament: a Semantic Study* (1945): and, for the suggested connexion with the Accadian têrtu, 'dispatch, message, injunction' (cf. wa'āru, I. 1, 'to go, set out', II. 1, 'to dispatch, enjoin'), see the discussion of the etymology of the foregoing Hebrew terms by Östborn, op. cit., pp. 4–22; also I. Engnell, *Israel and the Law*, S.B.U. 7 (1954), pp. 1–16.

[2] This is best illustrated by the text of 1 Sam. xiv. 41 as restored on the basis of LXX: cf., for example, S. R. Driver, *Notes on the Hebrew Text and the Topography of the Books of Samuel*, 2nd edit. rev. (1913), *in loc.* It may be noted, however, that the term אוּרִים is perhaps to be derived, not from √אוֹר, 'to give light' (as in R.V. mgn. on Exod. xxviii. 30, i.e. 'Lights'), but from √ארר, 'to curse'; it would then suggest the corresponding disintegration (cf. Num. v. 11–31 (P); Ps. cix. 17 f.). The term תֻּמִּים, as is generally recognized, is derived from √תמם, 'to be complete'; it therefore suggests a corresponding integrity. Hence, at the first test in the example cited, if the guilt rests with Saul and Jonathan, the former is to receive the answer in the form of the Urim; but, if the people are guilty, Saul is to receive the answer in the form of the Tummim, i.e. he and Jonathan are without fault. Cf. J. Wellhausen, *Prolegomena zur Geschichte Israels = Geschichte Israels*, i, 2nd edit. (1883), p. 419, n. 1, E.T. by J. S. Black and A. Menzies, *Prolegomena to the History of Israel* (1885), p. 394 n., followed, for example, by F. Schwally, *Z.A.W.* xi (1891), p. 172, and G. F. Moore, *E.B.* iv (1903), art. 'Urim and Thummim'. This seems much more likely than the attempts to link the Hebrew אוּרִים with what is thought to be a corresponding root in Accadian. Cf. (a) W. Muss-Arnolt, 'The Urim and Thummim', *A.J.S.L.* xvi (1899–1900), pp. 218 f., who thinks in terms of ûrtu, 'command' (cf. wa'āru, II. 1, 'to dispatch, enjoin', as cited in the previous note): (b) Dhorme, op. cit., p. 237, who cites wa'āru, I. 1, in its meaning 'to set out' (see again the previous note) with a view to linking the two Hebrew forms אוּרִים and תֻּמִּים in terms of the 'beginning' and 'end' of an inquiry.

the law, so to speak, concerning מִשְׁפָּטִים, i.e. 'rules' governing civil and criminal causes,[1] and תּוֹרָה, i.e. 'direction' in
matters of ceremonial observance.[2] It points to a legal code
representing the accumulated experience of the past[3] and
covering the realm of both civil and 'religious' law; for in
Israel there was no such clear distinction as that between
jus and *fas*.[4]

Such giving of תּוֹרָה or 'direction', particularly in matters
of ceremonial observance, thus came to be the mark of the
priestly office.[5] Towards the close of the eighth century, for
example, Micah complains that in Jerusalem, just as the
civil head can be influenced in his ruling or judgement by
means of a bribe, and just as the prophet practises divination[6] for its monetary value, so the priest places his legal
direction upon a cash basis;[7] and a century or so later there
are still three outstanding means of securing guidance in
the various walks of life—the advice of an elder, the observation[8] of a prophet, and the תּוֹרָה of a priest.[9] Ezekiel likewise denounces the priests of his day for their abuse of תּוֹרָה
in that they have failed to distinguish between the sacred and
the profane, the unclean and the clean;[10] and finally, for
example, Haggai has left an instructive picture from the
early post-exilic period of the way in which he sought a

[1] Cf., for example (despite J. Begrich, 'Die priesterliche Tora', in *Werden und Wesen des Alten Testaments*, ed. J. Hempel, B.Z.A.W. 66 (1936), pp. 63–88), S. R. Driver, *Deuteronomy*, I.C.C., 3rd edit. (1902), pp. 401 f.; Gray, op. cit., pp. 219 ff.; M. Haller, *R.G.G.*² v (1931), art. 'Tora': and see further Hempel, *Die althebräische Literatur*, pp. 73 ff.

[2] Cf., for example, Driver, loc. cit.; Haller, loc. cit.: and see further Eiss-feldt, op. cit., pp. 31 ff., 84 f.

[3] Gray, loc. cit.

[4] Cf. Oesterley and Robinson, op. cit., p. 32.

[5] The term תּוֹרָה, however, is not restricted to the work of the priest: it is also used with reference to (*a*) that of the prophet or seer, e.g. 2 Kings xvii. 13; Isa. i. 10, viii. 16 ff., xxx. 8 ff. (as below, p. 11); Jer. xxvi. 4 ff.; Zech. vii. 12; (*b*) that of the teacher of 'wisdom', e.g. Prov. i. 8, iii. 1, iv. 2, vi. 20, 23, vii. 2, xiii. 14, xxxi. 26. See further, with regard to the last point, Östborn, op. cit., pp. 112 ff.   [6] See below, pp. 31 ff.   [7] iii. 9–12.

[8] See below, pp. 11 ff., 36 ff., on this intentionally ambiguous rendering.

[9] Ezek. vii. 26: cf. Jer. xviii. 18.

[10] xxii. 26: cf. Zeph. iii. 4.

תּוֹרָה or verdict from the contemporary priesthood of the second Temple on just such a type of question.[1]

Further, it was in virtue of this aspect of his office that the priest was eventually able to claim certain monopolies as the representative of the people—notably in the matter of service at Yahweh's altar. In early times the head of a household[2] (or even a junior member in the person of a son),[3] a judge,[4] a prophet,[5] or finally, for example, the king[6] is found offering sacrifice at many a different spot. Already in the 'Blessing of Moses', however, the service at the altar could be classed as a Levitical (priestly) function;[7] and in the later legislation, associated with the cultus of the Jerusalem Temple and its claim to a monopoly of worship, it is a priestly prerogative.[8] Hence, as a result of the emphasis laid upon such ritual in the second Temple,[9] one is apt to regard the carrying out of sacrificial duties as the primary function of the priest, and so to overlook the important fact that within his own sphere he was originally as much a medium of revelation as the prophet. Indeed it is a prophet of the post-exilic period[10] who emphasizes this priestly responsibility with the memorable words:[11]

> The lips of a priest should guard knowledge,
> And direction (תּוֹרָה) should one seek at his mouth;
> For he is the Messenger of Yahweh of Hosts.

What one has to stress, then, is the fact that the role of the priest was thus a dual one. He was not only the representative of the people before Yahweh; he was also Yahweh's spokesman. At the same time, as already indicated, such

---

[1] ii. 10 ff.   [2] e.g. Judges xiii. 19; Job i. 5.   [3] Judges vi. 19 ff.
[4] e.g. 1 Sam. vii. 7 ff.   [5] See below, p. 27.
[6] e.g. 2 Sam. vi. 12 f., 17 ff. (cf. 1 Chron. xvi. 1 ff.), xxiv. 18–25 (1 Chron. xxi. 18–xxii. 1); 1 Kings iii. 4, 15 (2 Chron. i. 6). Cf., in general, A. George, 'Fautes contre Yahweh dans les Livres de Samuel', *R.B.* liii (1946), pp. 172 f.
[7] See above, pp. 5 f.   [8] See above, p. 4.   [9] Cf. Gray, op. cit., pp. 237 f.
[10] See below, pp. 64 f.
[11] Mal. ii. 7 (cf. Hos. iv. 6; 2 Chron. xv. 3). For something of the significance to be found even in such a reference to the כֹּהֵן or 'priest' as the 'Messenger' (מַלְאָךְ) of Yahweh, see the writer's monograph, *The One and the Many in the Israelite Conception of God* (1942), pp. 36 ff., 2nd edit. (1961), pp. 32 ff.

divine knowledge as he possessed was derived either from a form of divination or from his training in the accumulated experience of the past.

II

The כֹּהֵן or 'priest', however, was not the only type of cultic specialist. As is shown by the story of Saul's first meeting with Samuel, the רֹאֶה or (as this term is traditionally and indeed literally rendered) the 'seer' is also represented as filling such a role.[1]

Now it may be recalled that the narrative in question contains an oft-quoted note to the effect that:[2]

Formerly in Israel, when he went to consult God, a man would say, 'Come, let us go to the רֹאֶה'. For the נָבִיא of today was formerly called a רֹאֶה.

The value of this note, however, must not be exaggerated; for, as it stands, it is ambiguous. Thus, taken in isolation from its context, it does not even make it clear that originally two types of individual were distinguished by the respective terms. Nevertheless the very existence of the two forms may be held to suggest that such was the case; and this is confirmed by the narrative to which the note belongs.[3] Even so, however, the most that one is justified in saying is that at the time of the writer the use of the term נָבִיא had supplanted that of רֹאֶה;[4] the passage does not imply that the רֹאֶה, as a type, had disappeared. Indeed a possible interpretation of the passage is that the רֹאֶה proper had survived—but under the name of the נָבִיא who, in the earlier form, no longer existed. In short, the only conclusion that one may draw from the above note is that in course of time the term נָבִיא had secured a certain extension in meaning.

What, then, was the original distinction between the נָבִיא

---

[1] See 1 Sam. ix. 1–x. 16.   [2] ix. 9.   [3] x. 5 ff.
[4] Cf. A. Lods, *Israël des origines au milieu du VIIIe siècle* (1930), pp. 513 f., E.T. by S. H. Hooke, *Israel from its Beginnings to the Middle of the Eighth Century* (1932), pp. 442 f.

and the רֹאֶה? The former (i.e. the early type) is often, indeed commonly, described as an 'ecstatic'—a term which admits a wide range of meaning. For example, it has been argued that, in so far as he possessed supernatural knowledge, the נָבִיא (as an 'ecstatic') secured this through the temporary excitation of his own mental powers in such a way as to give rise to a 'vision'.[1] On this theory the רֹאֶה, in contrast with the נָבִיא, obtained his superior knowledge, not in such a state of 'ecstasy', but by means of 'external observations and perceptions, preferably the illusions of nocturnal gloom, the half-awake state and dream'. In short, he was an interpreter of signs and portents, like the Babylonian bārû, the Greek οἰωνοσκόπος, and the Roman *auspex*.[2] The evidence adduced, however, is far too vague and circumstantial to justify so nice a distinction, which seems rather artificial. It involves too restricted a use of the term 'vision' which, besides being applied without prejudice as to the part which may be played by normal sense impressions,[3] should also be allowed to include auditory and other phenomena.[4] Moreover, one may hardly overlook the fact (despite its apparent inevitability) that all the outstanding examples of visions in a literal sense, such as that of the 'witch' of En-dor,[5] that of Elisha and his servant at Dothan,[6] Micaiah's

---

[1] G. Hölscher, *Die Profeten* (1914), pp. 125 ff.

[2] Hölscher, loc. cit.

[3] As Hölscher himself recognizes, of course; op. cit., pp. 45 ff.

[4] See, for example, T. K. Oesterreich, *R.G.G.*[2] ii (1928), art. 'Ekstase': and cf. T. H. Robinson, *Prophecy and the Prophets in Ancient Israel* (1923), 2nd edit. rev. (1953), pp. 41 ff.; Lods, loc. cit. Despite the now common practice of using the terms 'ecstasy' and 'ecstatic' to define the function of the early נָבִיא, the reader will find that they are consistently avoided from now on so far as this monograph is concerned; for, unless one's use of these terms is carefully defined, confusion seems bound to arise. Cf. A. Guillaume, *Prophecy and Divination* (1938), pp. 290 ff.: and see further, for example, W. R. Inge, *E.R.E.* v (1912), art. 'Ecstasy'; J. B. Pratt, *The Religious Consciousness* (1920), chaps. xvi–xx; Oesterreich, loc. cit. See also p. 18, n. 4: and cf. now the comment by H. H. Rowley, *The Servant of the Lord and Other Essays on the Old Testament*, p. 93, who rightly objects that 'there is commonly a looseness and want of definition in the use of the word "ecstasy"'.

[5] 1 Sam. xxviii. 12 ff.

[6] 2 Kings vi. 17.

vision of the heavenly Court,[1] Isaiah's Temple vision,[2] the visions of Amos,[3] Jeremiah,[4] Ezekiel,[5] and Zechariah[6] (as also those recorded in the Hebrew sections of the book of Daniel),[7] are introduced by the verb of which רֹאֶה is the active participle *Qal*; and the cognate terms מַרְאָה[8] and מַרְאֶה[9] may also be used of such literal visions.

Here it is opportune to note that the term חֹזֶה, which may also be rendered more or less literally as 'seer', is usually regarded as synonymous with רֹאֶה.[10] Thus, in a passage from Isaiah (which incidentally illustrates the fact that the latter term was still in use towards the close of the eighth century B.C.),[11] they are presented as follows in what may be regarded as a piece of synonymous parallelism:[12]

For it is a rebellious people, deceitful children,
Children who will not listen to the direction (תּוֹרָה) of Yahweh,
Who say to the רֹאִים, 'We do not want you to see—'
And to the חֹזִים, 'We do not want you to observe—what is right.
Speak to us smooth things!
Observe deceitful things!'

[1] 1 Kings xxii. 19 ff. (cf. 17 f.): see also 2 Chron. xviii. 16 ff.
[2] vi. 1 ff.   [3] vii. 1–9, ix. 1 ff.: cf. viii. 1–3.
[4] iv. 23 ff.: cf. i. 11 ff., xxiv. 1 ff.   [5] e.g. i. 1 ff., viii. 1 ff.
[6] i–vi.   [7] viii–xii.
[8] Ezek. viii. 4, xi. 24, xliii. 3; Dan. viii. 16, 26, 27, ix. 23, x. 1.
[9] e.g. Ezek. i. 1, viii. 3, xl. 2; Dan. x. 7, 8, 16. In 1 Sam. iii. 15 מַרְאָה is used of a purely auditory experience. Cf. Gen. xlvi. 2 (E) and Num. xii. 6 (E); but note that in these two cases the lack of detail involves ambiguity. The same may be said of רֹאֶה (EVV. 'vision') in Isa. xxviii. 7.
[10] J. Lindblom, *Profetismen i Israel* (1934), pp. 146 f., suggests that originally רֹאֶה may have been the more vulgar and חֹזֶה the more cultured term.
[11] See above, p. 9. The form רֹאֶה is found elsewhere with certainty only in 1 Chron. ix. 22, xxvi. 28, xxix. 29; 2 Chron. xvi. 7, 10. In 2 Sam. xv. 27 the doubtful reading הֲרֹאֶה) is at best a purely verbal form; and for רֹאֶה in Isa. xxviii. 7, see above, n. 9, *ad fin.* The term חֹזֶה occurs somewhat more often, its preservation in the books of Chronicles (like that of רֹאֶה) being a specially notable feature. It is to be found unquestionably in 2 Sam. xxiv. 11; 2 Kings xvii. 13; Amos vii. 12; Mic. iii. 7; Isa. xxix. 10, xxx. 10; 1 Chron. xxi. 9, xxv. 5, xxix. 29; 2 Chron. ix. 29, xii. 15, xix. 2, xxix. 25, 30, xxxiii. 18, xxxv. 15. Note also 2 Chron. xxxiii. 19 (LXX); and for Isa. xxviii. 15, see below, p. 13, n. 3.
[12] xxx. 9 f. For the significance of such parallelism, which is an established feature of Hebrew poetry, see, for example, Oesterley and Robinson, op. cit., pp. 139 ff.

Such parallelism, however, does not preclude the possibility that these two terms indicate two different types; and comparative study certainly suggests a slight difference of emphasis in the use of the two roots.[1] In short, √חזה seems to be used rather more than √ראה with reference to visions in the secondary sense of the term, i.e. of auditory rather than strictly visual phenomena.[2] Thus, as already pointed out above, all the outstanding examples of visions in a literal sense are introduced by the verbal form of √ראה; and, while it is true that Habakkuk, for example, can speak of being on the watch to see (לִרְאוֹת) what Yahweh may *say* to him, such a secondary use of this root is comparatively rare.[3] Similarly, while there is one clear example of the use of מַרְאָה with reference to a purely auditory experience,[4] the corresponding term מַרְאֶה seems never to be found in this restricted sense. On the other hand, an oracle may be introduced quite idiomatically, not merely as the חָזוֹן (tradi-

---

[1] Several attempts have been made to distinguish between √ראה and √חזה. Cf. J. Hänel, *Das Erkennen Gottes bei den Schriftpropheten*, B.W.A.T., N.F. 4 (1923), pp. 7 ff. The existence of these two roots, of course, illustrates the composite character of the Hebrew language, the latter representing an Aramaic strand (cf. G. R. Driver, *Problems of the Hebrew Verbal System*, O.T.S. 2 (1936), pp. 98 ff.); but this does not seem to have any bearing on the point under discussion. Cf. Rowley, op. cit., pp. 99 f., with special reference to M. A. van den Oudenrijn, 'De vocabulis quibusdam, termino נָבִיא synonymis', in *Biblica* vi (1925), pp. 294–311, 406–17, particularly 304 f.; also the latter's major work, נבואה: *De prophetiae charismate in populo israelitico* (1926), pp. 37 ff., esp. 47 f.

[2] Cf. the somewhat similar finding of Jepsen, op. cit., pp. 43–56, esp. 48 f., 52 f.; but note his further conclusion in the summary statement that חָזוֹן represents 'mehr eine Art *nächtlicher* Audition, nicht dagegen Vision im eigentlichen Sinne'. (Italics mine. A. R. J.) One must beware of laying too much emphasis, however, even upon what appear as auditory phenomena; the use of the Hebrew terminology may be quite formal. See below, pp. 47 ff. It should hardly be necessary to add that, as this is an historical rather than a psychological study, such an expression as 'auditory phenomena' is used without prejudice as to any theory of the mental processes involved.

[3] Hab. ii. 1. Cf. Num. xxiii. 3 ff. (JE): also, perhaps, 2 Kings viii. 10; Jer. xxiii. 18; Zech. i. 9; and, indeed, Jer. xxxviii. 21; Ezek. xi. 25 (although one should bear in mind the ambiguity of the term דָּבָר as denoting either 'word' or 'thing'. Cf. the variations in the EVV. as regards these two passages, and see below, pp. 36 ff.).

[4] See above, p. 11, n. 9.

tionally rendered by 'vision'), but also as the דָּבָר ('word') or מַשָּׂא ('utterance'),[1] which so-and-so 'observed' (חָזָה).[2] Similarly, the story of Samuel's auditory experience as a youth at Shiloh is introduced by the statement that in those days the דָּבָר of Yahweh was rare; there was no outbreak of חָזוֹן.[3] In fact, the terms דָּבָר and חָזוֹן are more or less

---

[1] See below, p. 40, n. 4, *ad fin.*

[2] For חָזוֹן, see Isa. i. 1: cf. Ezek. xii. 27 (but note the context, and see below, p. 37), xiii. 16. For דָּבָר, see Isa. ii. 1; Amos i. 1; Mic. i. 1. For מַשָּׂא, see Isa. xiii. 1; Hab. i. 1: cf. Lam. ii. 14. The parallel with the use of חָזוֹן and especially with that of מַשָּׂא shows that in such cases דָּבָר must mean 'word'; it can hardly mean 'thing', although it may carry with it the significance of subject-matter with reference to some form of vision. See below, p. 37.

[3] 1 Sam. iii. 1. Cf. the use of the cognate forms (i) חָזוּת, in Isa. xxi. 2, xxix. 11: (ii) חִזָּיוֹן, in 2 Sam. vii. 17 (= חָזוֹן in the corresponding passage, 1 Chron. xvii. 15): (iii) מַחֲזֶה, in Gen. xv. 1 (JE); Num. xxiv. 4, 16 (JE); Ezek. xiii. 7. Indeed, with the exception of Isa. xxix. 7, the unmistakable use of חָזוֹן with reference to a vision in the literal sense of the term seems to be limited to the book of Daniel, e.g. viii, *passim.* The exact significance of the terms חֹזֶה and חָזוּת in Isa. xxviii. 15 and 18 respectively remains a matter of dispute, although the fact that A.V., R.V., and R.S.V. render both terms uniformly by 'agreement' is some indication of the steady recognition that both these terms are virtually synonymous with the parallel term בְּרִית, 'covenant'. Cf., for example, R.S.V.: (*a*) 'We have made a covenant (בְּרִית) with death, and with Sheol we have an agreement (חֹזֶה).' (*b*) 'Then your covenant (בְּרִית) with death will be annulled, and your agreement (חָזוּת) with Sheol will not stand.' The attempt to take חֹזֶה in a personal sense as the familiar term for 'seer' and to think accordingly of a prophet who is responsible for maintaining the implied agreement with Sheol (cf., for example, G. Hoffmann, *Z.A.W.* iii (1883), p. 95, n. 2, followed by C. Siegfried and B. Stade, *Hebräisches Wörterbuch zum Alten Testamente* (1893), s.v.) has been rightly regarded as unsatisfactory. Cf., for example, R. Kraetzschmar, *Die Bundesvorstellung im Alten Testament in ihrer geschichtlichen Entwickelung* (1896), p. 52, n. 6: 'doch passt dann das persönliche חֹזֶה schlecht zu dem sächlichen ברית.' On the assumption that חֹזֶה may denote 'vision' (or should be read as חֹזֶה or emended to חָזוּת, as in verse 18, in order to secure this meaning), the supposed connexion of both חֹזֶה and חָזוּת with the root under discussion (i.e. √חזה = Arabic حزى) has been defended in terms of (i) a necromantic manifestation of some kind, and (ii) the phenomena of divination or augury, especially as used in connexion with the making of treaties, and so by metonymy such a 'treaty' or 'covenant'. Cf., for example, (*a*) B. Duhm, H.K., 4th edit. rev. (1922), *in loc.*: (*b*) F. Hitzig, *Der Prophet Jesaja* (1833), F. Buhl, *Jesaja* (1894), J. A. Montgomery, *J.B.L.* xxxi (1912), pp. 142 f., and O. Procksch, K.A.T. (1930), *in loc.*; E. König, *Hebräisches und aramäisches Wörterbuch zum Alten Testament*, 6th and 7th edit. (1936), s.v. While none of this is very convincing, a connexion with √חזה (= حزى) remains possible,

synonymous when used with reference to oracular functions; so that on such occasions חָזוֹן may, perhaps, be rendered more appropriately by 'observation' than by the somewhat stronger word 'vision'.[1]

Nevertheless the above distinction between the two roots ראה and חזה may not be pressed—at least so far as the nominal use of the active participle *Qal* is concerned. Thus (again in the eighth century B.C.) Amos could be addressed by Amaziah, priest of the royal sanctuary at Bethel, as a חֹזֶה;[2] yet, as already noticed[3] and, indeed, as is shown by the particular incident under discussion,[4] he was subject on occasion to visions in the literal sense of the term. On the other hand, Samuel is credited with visions of a secondary kind, i.e. auditory phenomena; yet in the same narrative he is described as a רֹאֶה.[5]

if one may think of these two terms as implying something like 'foresight', the parallel with בְּרִית being explained in terms of making 'provision' for the future: cf. the way in which we speak of the 'provisions' of a treaty. On the other hand, there is much force in the suggestion that we should think, rather, of √חזה = Arabic حَاذَى, III, 'to be opposite to, confront', VI, 'to confront one another'; and in that case we may have a parallel to 'covenant' in terms of something like a 'rapprochement'. Cf. G. R. Driver, *J.T.S.* xxxviii (1937), p. 44, followed by F. Zorell, *Lexicon Hebraicum et Aramaicum Veteris Testamenti* (1946–), s.v. Finally, L. Köhler, *Z.A.W.* xlviii (1930), pp. 227 f. (cf. K.B., s.v.), would emend the text in each case by resorting to the term חֶסֶד, which is commonly used with reference to one's obligations in connexion with a 'covenant' (cf. N. H. Snaith, *The Distinctive Ideas of the Old Testament* (1944), pp. 94 ff., and the writer's own discussion of this term as cited above, p. 5, n. 6); but it seems most unlikely that √חסד should have been confused with √חזה twice in such close connexion. Moreover the M.T. appears to have the support of the ancient versions; and this remains true even though LXX renders חָזוּת by means of ἐλπίς (perhaps as implying something to which one 'looks forward') rather than συνθήκη or διαθήκη (cf. verse 15).

[1] Cf. the range of meaning in the English expression, 'to make an observation'. See further (paying particular attention to the context) Jer. xiv. 14; Ezek. vii. 13; Hab. ii. 2; 1 Chron. xvii. 15: and especially Jer. xxiii. 16; Ezek. vii. 26, xii. 21–28; Hos. xii. 11 (EVV. 10); Prov. xxix. 18, as discussed below, pp. 36 ff. Cf., too, the statement made by A. B. Davidson, *Old Testament Prophecy* (1903), p. 137, in discussing the term חֹזֶה: 'We must hold that the word was used with all the latitude with which we employ the word "see". It is quite false to restrict it to what we technically call a "vision".'

[2] Amos vii. 12.   [3] See above, p. 11, n. 3.   [4] Verses 7 ff.
[5] 1 Sam. ix. 1–x. 16; see esp. ix. 15, 17.

It thus appears that the רֹאֶה and the חֹזֶה (if ever any distinction was observed in practice, and this is extremely doubtful) were credited with extraordinary experiences of both a (literally) visual and an auditory kind. This is not to say, of course, that the seer's powers of observation were limited to such experiences. It may well be that, like the later (and, for all one may know, the earlier) נָבִיא or prophet,[1] he used to practise divination, and that accordingly his assets included any means of 'seeing' or 'observing' things hidden from the knowledge of ordinary men.[2] Similarly it must remain an open question as to whether or not his extraordinary experiences were ever the result of artificial stimulation.[3] Two facts, however, are certain and must be emphasized. The narrative of 1 Samuel ix. 1–x. 16 makes it clear, in the first place, that the seer could be consulted for the sake of his unusual and divinely gifted powers,[4] and that, to this extent at least,[5] he must have had them under his control. Secondly, in view of the fact that Samuel had charge of the sacrifice at the local 'high place',[6] it is obvious that the seer was a cultic figure of some importance with a special responsibility for the formal worship of Yahweh. Indeed confirmation of this may be found in the fact that it was Gad the חֹזֶה, also called a נָבִיא,[7] who bade David set up an altar in the threshing-floor of Araunah the Jebusite; and it was clearly Gad's intention that the king should seek Yahweh's forgiveness (i.e. for taking a census of the people) by means of a definite cultic act—that of sacrifice.[8] Moreover (and this is ultimately very significant),[9] according to 2 Chronicles xxix. 25, Yahweh's original commandment concerning the musical service of the Jerusalem Temple was made known through the agency of this same Gad, the

---

[1] See below, pp. 31 ff.
[2] Cf. Lods, op. cit., pp. 513 f., E.T., p. 443.
[3] See below, pp. 17 ff.   [4] Cf. again ix. 9.   [5] See below, p. 22, n. 3.
[6] See below, p. 29, n. 2, *ad fin.*   [7] See below, p. 71.
[8] 2 Sam. xxiv. 11, 18; cf. 1 Chron. xxi. 9, 18: and, in defence of an early date for the former passage, see J. M. P. Smith, *The Prophets and Their Times*, 2nd edit. rev. by W. A. Irwin (1941), pp. 28 ff.
[9] See below, pp. 69 ff.

royal חֹזֶה, in association with David the king and Nathan the
נָבִיא.[1]

As for the early נָבִיא, some of the most valuable evidence
for an understanding of his person and work is contained
(like that for the role of the seer) in the stories of Samuel
and Saul. Thus one learns that,[2] as the latter was returning
from his first encounter with Samuel, he met a 'string'[3] of
נְבִיאִים descending from a local sanctuary to the accompaniment of various musical instruments and, at the same time,
exhibiting the behaviour characteristic of their class; they
were 'acting (*or* playing) the נָבִיא'.[4] The effect of the meeting
is (so to speak) electric; for Saul is immediately seized with
similar behaviour—so much so that he loses his own identity
and is 'turned into another man'. In the phraseology of the
passage, 'the divine רוּחַ ("Spirit") comes tearing upon him',[5]
so that he 'acts the נָבִיא'.[6] It was this event, one is told,
which gave rise to the proverb,[7] 'Is Saul also among the
נְבִיאִים?'; and the context suggests that the latter were apt
to be objects of contempt.[8] Another story,[9] equally illuminating, offers a different explanation of the origin of the
proverb. David has fled from Saul and taken refuge with
Samuel in Ramah. Saul thereupon sends messengers to
seize the fugitive; but on their arrival they find Samuel
apparently presiding over a veteran group of נְבִיאִים[10]

---

[1] See below, p. 71.   [2] 1 Sam. x. 5–13.   [3] חֶבֶל.

[4] הִתְנַבֵּא: cf. G.K. § 54*d*.

[5] For a discussion of the use of √צלח in such a context, see M. Buber,
Königtum Gottes, 3rd edit. rev. (1956), p. 220 (i.e. p. 142, n. 75).

[6] See further, for example, Hänel, op. cit., pp. 161 ff.; F. Haeussermann,
Wortempfang und Symbol in der alttestamentlichen Prophetie, B.Z.A.W. 58
(1932), pp. 24 ff.; and, in warning against the now prevalent view that in
such a case the רוּחַ of Yahweh was thought of as an impersonal force, the
writer's work, *The One and the Many in the Israelite Conception of God*,
pp. 17 ff., 2nd edit., pp. 13 ff., also *The Vitality of the Individual in the Thought
of Ancient Israel* (1949), pp. 34 ff.   [7] מָשָׁל: see below, p. 40, n. 4.

[8] This remained true of at least a certain type of נָבִיא: 2 Kings ix. 11;
Zech. xiii. 2–6. Cf. the attitude of the Rwala Bedouin to their seers: A.
Musil, *The Manners and Customs of the Rwala Bedouins* (1928), p. 401.

[9] 1 Sam. xix. 18–24.

[10] For the expression לַהֲקַת הַנְּבִיאִים, see G. R. Driver, *J.T.S.* xxix
(1927–8), p. 394, and E. Ullendorff, *V.T.* vi (1956), p. 194.

engaged in their characteristic activity. As in the previous story, the meeting is (so to speak) electric in its effect; for the divine רוּחַ or 'Spirit' is said to come over the messengers, and they likewise 'act the נָבִיא'. Saul, learning what has taken place, sends more messengers—with a similar result. This happens a third time. Saul himself thereupon sets out for Ramah, but he is seized with similar behaviour even before he reaches his destination. On his arrival he strips himself of his clothes, joins in the general activity, and ends up by lying naked on the ground for the greater part of a day.

The immediate historical value of the second narrative is somewhat uncertain. It reflects a more favourable attitude to the נְבִיאִים, and is apparently the product of a later date than the former.[1] Nevertheless one may be sure that it gives an equally faithful picture of the general characteristics of this quite extraordinary class of people. Samuel, significantly, is no longer a רֹאֶה or 'seer' but a נָבִיא. As such he is a member and, indeed, the leader of an organized group; he has his disciples. Such organization into groups known as the 'sons'[2] of a נָבִיא or of the נְבִיאִים is to be noted; for there is direct evidence that it was a regular feature until late in the monarchical period.[3] Further, it is obvious from both accounts that the characteristic behaviour of the נָבִיא was of a frenzied kind; and this is confirmed by the fact that the verbal form used to describe it is found as a parallel to that which means 'to be frenzied, fanatic *or* mad'.[4] Indeed it was always possible, apparently, for a נָבִיא of this type to

---

[1] Cf., for example, H. P. Smith, I.C.C. (1899); A. R. S. Kennedy, Cent.B. (n.d.); P. (E.) Dhorme, E.B. (1910); H. Gressmann, S.A.T. ii. 1, 2nd edit. rev. (1921); S. Mowinckel, G.T.M.M.M. ii (1935); R. de Vaux, S.B.J. 2nd edit. rev. (1961): all *in loc.*

[2] For the use of the term בֵּן to denote a community, see J. Pedersen, *Israel: its Life and Culture I–II* (1926), 2nd edit. with additions (1959), pp. 53 f. On the other hand, it has been suggested in the light of Assyro-Babylonian and Bedouin parallels that the Hebrew terminology should be taken more literally, i.e. as implying the existence of prophetic groups of an hereditary type. Cf. Guillaume, op. cit., p. 124.

[3] Cf. 1 Kings xxii; 2 Kings i ff.; Amos vii. 14: also Jer. xxxv. 4. See below, p. 62. [4] Jer. xxix. 26.

be described as a fanatic or madman.[1] Madness, however, is commonly regarded in the East and elsewhere as a mark of contact with the divine (or the demonic) world;[2] so that such נְבִיאִים probably would not quarrel with this equation. Nay, more: there can be no reasonable doubt that, where they are found acting in this way, their behaviour (in so far as it is not merely simulated) is due for the most part (but not necessarily in every individual case)[3] to artificial stimulation designed expressly to bring about an abnormal (not to say 'ecstatic')[4] experience which should prove to

[1] Cf. 2 Kings ix. 11.

[2] Cf., for example, E. W. Lane, *The Manners and Customs of the Modern Egyptians*, 5th edit. (1860), in the Everyman's Library edition, pp. 234 f.; E. Westermarck, *Ritual and Belief in Morocco* (1926), i, pp. 47 ff.: see also n. 4, *ad fin.*

[3] See below, p. 22, n. 3.

[4] See above, p. 10, n. 4. In thus using the description 'abnormal', rather than 'ecstatic', the writer is following the practice advocated by H. W. Robinson, 'The Psychology and Metaphysic of "Thus saith Yahweh"', *Z.A.W.* xli (1923), p. 2; *Redemption and Revelation* (1942), p. 140. On the other hand, while agreeing with the desirable distinction between 'ecstasy' and 'possession', the writer is unable to accept the further suggestion that the former term, as being of Greek origin, is unsuitable for dealing with the phenomena of Hebrew psychology (i.e. on the ground that the Hebrew conception of man is that of an animated body rather than an incarnate soul). Op. cit., pp. 134 ff.: cf., too, Guillaume, op. cit., p. 291, n. 1. In fact it seems to the present writer that the word 'ecstasy' may be used quite fittingly in such a connexion, if it be correlated with 'possession' in terms of a polarity within the general conception of 'corporate personality' as applied to both man and God, i.e. if the term 'ecstasy' be used of the reaching out of the נֶפֶשׁ toward the divine (by way of an 'extension' of the human personality operating beyond the contour of the body), while the term 'possession' is used of the reverse process—the influx or influence of the divine upon man (by way of the רוּחַ or 'Spirit' of Yahweh operating as the extended Personality of the Godhead). See again *The One and the Many in the Israelite Conception of God*, esp. pp. 6 ff., 19 f., and 36 ff., 2nd edit., pp. 2 ff., 15 f., 32 ff. One may think of Israelite psychology as revealing a fluctuation between these two poles—not altogether unlike the modern example from Upper Egypt which is furnished by W. S. Blackman. A young man, who had been in a state of violent madness for some three months, was being treated for his trouble by a sheikh who had declared him to be 'possessed by an *'afrīt* [i.e. a demon]'. After various preliminaries, including the burning of incense and the recitation of some magical sentences, 'the sheikh finally told the *'afrīt* to leave the man, but he replied (of course speaking through the man), "From what part of his body shall I leave him? May I come out through one of his eyes . . .?" The sheikh replied that he would not permit him to do this, but

be the means of obtaining divine guidance in the affairs
of life.

This is made clear in the story of the four hundred or so
נְבִיאִים consulted by Ahab in company with Jehoshaphat
prior to the attack upon Ramoth-gilead.[1] The נְבִיאִים in
question are described as exhibiting the above characteristic
behaviour, apparently under the leadership of Zedekiah;[2]
and the narrative shows that in so doing they were acting as
the spokesmen of Yahweh. Moreover, the whole purpose
of the meeting was that Ahab might 'seek the דְּבַר (or
"Word")[3] of Yahweh';[4] and therefore the very fact that the
נְבִיאִים were summoned for consultation shows that their
behaviour must have been artificially promoted for the
occasion. Again, the first narrative mentioned above[5] indicates that music, as one might expect, was of considerable
importance in stimulating such behaviour; and fortunately
the Old Testament preserves a valuable illustration of its
use in this connexion.[6] Thus it appears that upon one occasion Jehoram, king of Israel, and Jehoshaphat, king of
Judah, together with the king of Edom, had united in an
attack upon Moab; but in the course of their campaign they
found themselves in difficulties on account of the grave
shortage of water. This drove them to seek a נָבִיא for the
purpose of securing divine guidance, and one was found in

that he was to come out of the big toe of one foot. The sheikh then placed a
ḳulleh [i.e. an earthenware water-bottle] on the ground, and said to the *'afrīt*,
"I shall know that you have left the man if you knock over this *ḳulleh*".
Presently, as he continued reading his incantations, the sheikh saw a few
drops of blood fly from the man's big toe toward the *ḳulleh*, which was
immediately flung with a crash against the wall. The madman then sat up
and said, "Where am I? And who are you?" After a while he recognized all
his relatives, whom he had not known during the whole period of his madness. They asked him where he had been, to which he replied, "I have been
among the *'afārīt*".'—*The Fellāḥīn of Upper Egypt* (1927), pp. 231 ff. Note
the striking transition in the last sentence.

[1] I Kings xxii: cf. 2 Chron. xviii.
[2] See below, pp. 39 f.
[3] See below, pp. 37 ff.
[4] Verse 5.
[5] i.e. 1 Sam. x. 5–13.
[6] 2 Kings iii. 6 ff.

the person of Elisha. The latter, having been persuaded to function, called for music; and under its stimulation 'the Hand of Yahweh descended upon him',[1] so that he was able to give the required advice and thus deliver the royal allies from their plight.

Now it is to be observed that this represents no isolated phenomenon in the history of mankind, but one which may be illustrated over a wide area from early times until the present day.[2] Thus, in the ancient world a close parallel may be found in Elijah's opponents, the נְבִיאִים attached to the cultus of the Tyrian Baal,[3] and in the wandering 'priests' of the Dea Syria described by Apuleius.[4] Coming to more recent times one may quote the example of the so-called 'wizards' of Patagonia in the eighteenth century A.D.,[5] the *dugganawa* among the Veddas of Ceylon,[6] the *kuranmaran* of the Saoras of Orissa,[7] the shamans of Siberia,[8] the oracle-priests of Tibet,[9] and the dervishes and similar religious orders of North Africa and the Near East.[10] In every case

---

[1] For the terminology, see Haeussermann, op. cit., pp. 22 ff.; also *The Vitality of the Individual in the Thought of Ancient Israel*, p. 56, n. 1.

[2] The ensuing references may be supplemented from the valuable material for comparative purposes which may be found in the important trilogy by P. de Félice, *Poisons sacrés, ivresses divines* (1936); *Foules en délire, extases collectives* (1947); *L'Enchantement des danses et la magie du verbe* (1957). Cf., too, the equally important collection of comparative data in M. Eliade, *Le Chamanisme et les techniques archaïques de l'extase* (1951); also the brief but important general survey of the whole subject offered by N. K. Chadwick, *Poetry and Prophecy* (1942).

[3] 1 Kings xviii.

[4] *Metamorphoses* viii–ix.

[5] Cf. T. Falkner, *A Description of Patagonia &c.* (1774), pp. 116 f.

[6] Cf. C. G. and B. Z. Seligmann, *The Veddas* (1911), pp. 128 ff.

[7] Cf. V. Elwin, *The Religion of an Indian Tribe* (1955), pp. 128 ff., 469 ff.

[8] Cf., for example, V. M. Mikhailovskii, 'Shamanism in Siberia &c.', *J.A.I.* xxiv (1895), pp. 62–100, 126–58; also A. F. Puukko, 'Ekstatische Propheten mit besonderer Berücksichtigung der finnisch-ugrischen Parallelen', *Z.A.W.* liii (1935), pp. 23–35.

[9] Cf. R. de Nebesky-Wojkowitz, *Oracles and Demons of Tibet. The Cult and Iconography of the Tibetan Protective Deities* (1956), pp. 428 ff., 546 ff.

[10] Cf., for example, Lane, op. cit., chaps. x, xxiv, and xxv, and in general J. P. Brown, *The Darvishes or Oriental Spiritualism* (1868), now available in an improved edition, with notes, by H. A. Rose (1927); also É. Dermenghem, *Le Culte des saints dans l'Islam maghrébin*, 5th edit. (1954), pp. 197 ff., 251 ff.

one may observe the conscious aim of recognized specialists
to secure communion with the spirit world, usually under
the stimulation of chant or dance—or both of these together. Sometimes other stimuli are employed. Thus the
desired state might be promoted by means of subterranean
vapours, if we may believe what was said in Roman times
about the Pythia at Delphi,[1] or by the aid of smoke from
burning juniper twigs as with the oracle-priests of Tibet
again,[2] or by the use of tobacco smoke or intoxicants as in
the case of the *mandwa* of the African Baganda[3] or the *piai*
of British Guiana.[4]

Perhaps the most interesting and valuable parallel, however, is to be found among the Rwala Bedouin of the
present day. In this case 'the seer maintains that he commu-
nicates with an angel, *malak*, who announces to him the
will of Allâh.[5] Such an angel, an intermediary between
Allâh and the sorcerer, is called *munâbi* or *mnâbi*,[6] spokesman. As a rule the *munâbi* appears in the shape of a rider
seated on a white mare. He tells the seer what to proclaim
in Allâh's name. . . . Besides the angel the seer's ancestors
also appear to him in the night between Thursday and
Friday, instructing him how to behave. Yet neither the
angel nor the ancestors ever appear without a thorough
preparation on the part of the seer. Every seer has his
disciples, *ṭallâbt as-sirr*, who are taught all the external per-
formances necessary to display if the *munâbi* is to appear.
They come to the seer on Thursday night, accompany him

---

[1] Cf., for example, E. Rohde, *Psyche*, 7th and 8th edit. (1921), ii, pp. 58 ff.,
E.T. by W. B. Hillis (1925), pp. 290 f.; but note that, as is indicated above
in the text, the evidence for such subterranean vapours comes only from late
writers. Cf. T. Dempsey, *The Delphic Oracle* (1918), pp. 57 ff.; and H. W.
Parke and D. E. W. Wormell, *The Delphic Oracle* (1956), i, pp. 19 ff., where
the theory that the Pythia's inspiration was caused by a vapour issuing from
an underground chasm is treated as being due to rationalistic invention.

[2] Cf. de Nebesky-Wojkowitz, loc. cit.

[3] Cf. J. Roscoe, *The Baganda* (1911), pp. 274 f.

[4] Cf. W. E. Roth, 'An Inquiry into the Animism and Folklore of the
Guiana Indians', *B.A.E.R.(W.)* xxx (1915), pp. 103–386, esp. 327 ff.

[5] Cf. the visions of Zechariah, i. 7–vi. 8.

[6] Cf. the Hebrew term נָבִיא, and see below, p. 24.

on his visits to the sick and on raids,[1] and join him when-
ever he commands them. One part of their duty is to carry
little drums and other musical instruments, *dfûf w-šîš* or
dirbâš. If the sorcerer wants to call the spokesman-angel to
him, he beckons to the disciples to play, while he himself
squats with his head bent down. After a while he begins to
move, stands up, stretches out his hands, jumps about, con-
torts his body, and puts his hands, feet, and even his head
close to the fire, clapping his hands. The Bedouins say of
this that he is just playing, *jel'ab*, but his disciples call it
yielding to the influence of the *islâm*, ecstasy. When his
enthusiasm reaches its climax, either Allâh's spokesman or
some of the seer's ancestors appear on the scene.'[2]

Of course the fact that the characteristic behaviour of the
נָבִיא was artificially promoted does not preclude the possibility of a spontaneous seizure on his part;[3] and it may be that,

---

[1] The נָבִיא was likewise in special request in times of sickness and war:
cf., for example, the incidents referred to above, pp. 19 f., and below, pp. 23 ff.
The ultimate significance of this point should become clear in the immediate
sequel to this work.

[2] Musil, op. cit., pp. 400 f. Cf., too (with special reference to the preceding
note), pp. 402 f.: 'War expeditions on a large scale are always accompanied
by a sorcerer who instructs the commander in anything he may undertake.
The latter asks the sorcerer's advice only on occasions when he is at a loss
what to do. Then the seer stimulates himself with music and works himself
into an ecstasy, which helps him hear the angel speak and proclaim the will
of Allâh. Very often a sorcerer is summoned to the bedside of a person who
is seriously ill. He comes either with all or a few of his disciples and settles
down in the tent as a regular guest. During the day, but especially in the
evening, he orders his disciples to play, while he squats by the fire with his
head wrapped up and his face in his hands, listening to the music. After a
while he begins to contort the upper part of his body, jumps up, seizes a small
drum, beats it wildly, circles around the fire, and, dancing around the patient,
raps him with the drum on the head and legs; then, throwing the drum aside,
he lies above the patient, supporting himself by the feet and hands, breathes
into his mouth and nostrils, kneels down, rubs the patient on the breast,
stomach, and back, jumps up, dances around, and then, lying on him again,
mumbles unintelligible words. Sometimes he cures the sick person by this
process; sometimes the patient dies.' The whole picture offers a striking
parallel to the part played by Elisha in the incident described above, pp. 19 f.,
and (with certain modifications) that played by both Elijah and Elisha in the
stories of their healing activities recorded in 1 Kings xvii. 17–24; 2 Kings
iv. 32–37.

[3] The statement made above in the text, which is reproduced from the

as in the case of the Patagonian 'wizards'[1] and the Siberian shamans,[2] for example, neurotic sufferers were regarded as especially suitable candidates for this office. Nevertheless there is no evidence to show that this was so; and the noted behaviour of Saul (who, as it appears elsewhere, was evidently subject to some kind of nervous disorder),[3] as well as that of his messengers, finds ready illustration in the effect which the *zikr* of the modern dervishes often has upon bystanders.[4]

Thus, as with the רֹאֶה, so with the early נְבִיאִים this fact is certain and must be emphasized: they, too, were consulted for the sake of their unusual powers and therefore, to this extent,[5] must have had them under their control. Saul, one may remember, was driven to seek the assistance of the 'witch' of En-dor because he could get no answer from Yahweh by means of dreams, or by the use of the sacred lot,[6] or through the medium of נְבִיאִים.[7] Similarly one may recall the way in which Jeroboam I sent his wife to consult the נָבִיא Ahijah at Shiloh, concerning the sickness of their son Abijah;[8] or that in which the נָבִיא Elijah rebuked Ahaziah for sending to consult Baalzebub, the god of Ekron, concerning his possible recovery from the accident

first edition without change, apparently needs to be emphasized, as some readers tend to overlook the fact that the writer has been concerned from the first to leave room even here for what is now commonly known as the 'charismatic' form of prophecy. Cf. (i) what is said in the preface to this monograph about the many-sided problem which is posed by the whole question of 'prophecy' in ancient Israel; and (ii) what the writer accordingly regards as the one-sided approach to the question at issue which is made by Eichrodt, op. cit., pp. 207 ff., where, as it seems to the writer, Eichrodt is merely reproducing the traditional over-simplification of the problem which, in part, it is the purpose of this monograph to oppose. See also p. 15, n. 5; p. 18, n. 3; and below, n. 5.

[1] Cf. Falkner, loc. cit.

[2] Cf. Mikhailovskii, op. cit., pp. 85 ff.; but note the cautionary remarks of Chadwick, op. cit., p. 65.

[3] 1 Sam. xvi. 14 ff., xviii. 10.

[4] Cf. Lane, loc. cit., e.g. pp. 455 f.

[5] See above, p. 22, n. 3.

[6] See above, pp. 5 f.

[7] 1 Sam. xxviii. 6, 15.

[8] 1 Kings xiv. 1 ff.

of falling from his roof-chamber—as if there were no God in Israel whose דְּבָר or 'Word' might be sought in such a connexion.[1]

It must remain an open question as to whether they were credited with superhuman knowledge derived from the study of omens, portents, and the like; but the foregoing evidence makes it clear that their characteristic behaviour was artificially promoted to this end—the aim being to secure an experience which might be interpreted as the influx of the divine רוּחַ or 'Spirit' (conceived in a personal, not impersonal, fashion),[2] as a result of which the נָבִיא was endowed with special oracular power. Hence there is no reason to reject the obvious etymology of the term נָבִיא which links it with the Accadian NABÛ[3] and the Arabic نَبَ;[4] and, this being the case, the traditional rendering 'prophet' (which corresponds to that of προφήτης in the Septuagint) may be accepted for working purposes as being also more or less a literal one.[5]

---

[1] 2 Kings i, esp. 3, 6, 16: cf. v. 1 ff., viii. 7 ff.

[2] See above, p. 16, n. 6.

[3] 'To call, name, announce'.

[4] I, 'to utter a sound' (e.g. 'to bark softly'); II, III, and IV, 'to inform, announce'. Cf. the *munâbi* or *mnâbi* mentioned above, pp. 21 f.

[5] This is to reject (a) the association of the term נָבִיא with √נבע as having reference to the 'welling up' or 'bubbling forth' of the divine message in the excitable condition suggested by the abnormal behaviour characteristic of this type of 'prophet', and (b) the theory that this term is a passive form of the verb בּוֹא, 'to enter', and thus denoted 'one who has been entered, possessed'. For the former view see, for example, W. Gesenius, *Thesaurus Linguae Hebraeae et Chaldaeae Veteris Testamenti*, ii. 2 (1840), p. 838a; H. Hackmann, 'Die geistigen Abnormitäten der alttestamentlichen Propheten', *N.T.T.* xxiii (1934), p. 42; O. Plöger, 'Priester und Prophet', *Z.A.W.* lxiii (1951), p. 170: and, for the latter suggestion, see J. P. N. Land, 'Over den godsnaam יהוה en den titel נביא', *T.T.* ii (1868), pp. 170–5; R. H. Pfeiffer, 'The Growth of Old Testament Religion' (reprinted from *The Shane Quarterly*, Jan. 1947), p. 15. Even so, however, the question remains as to whether the form is to be taken in an active or a passive sense. Cf. C. Brockelmann, *Grundriss der vergleichenden Grammatik der semitischen Sprachen*, i (1908), § 138. The former, with the resultant supposedly literal rendering 'speaker' or 'spokesman', is that which has been commonly accepted (as by Brockelmann, loc. cit.). Cf., for example, E. König, *Der Offenbarungsbegriff des Alten Testamentes*, i (1882), pp. 71 ff., esp. 75 ff., *Theologie des Alten Testaments*,

The early נָבִיא or 'prophet', then, had at least this much
in common with the priest (including the Levite) and the
seer: he was consulted for the sake of securing oracular
guidance. Accordingly there should be no cause for surprise
in the fact that (again like the priest, including the Levite,
and the seer) the prophet is found in close association with
cultus and sanctuary. In fact, while a prophet might be
consulted at any time or place in an emergency (whether at
his home[1] or while accompanying a military expedition[2]
for example), he was normally visited for such a purpose
on some festival day, such as the New Moon or Sabbath,
at the particular sanctuary to which he was permanently
attached or which he would obviously have occasion to

3rd and 4th edit. rev. (1923), pp. 50 ff., *Geschichte der alttestamentlichen
Religion*, 3rd and 4th edit. rev. (1924), pp. 132 f.; Davidson, op. cit.,
pp. 83 ff.; R. Kittel, *Geschichte des Volkes Israel*, ii, 6th and 7th edit. (1925),
p. 329; L. Dürr, *Wollen und Wirken der alttestamentlichen Propheten* (1926),
pp. 3 f.; Junker, op. cit., p. 36; Buber, op. cit., pp. 135 f., 218 f. (i.e. p. 136,
n. 63), but see below; T. J. Meek, *Hebrew Origins*, 2nd edit. rev. (1950),
pp. 150 f.; Smith and Irwin, op. cit., pp. 3 f.; Eichrodt, op. cit., p. 206.
Nevertheless see W. R. Smith, *The Prophets of Israel*, pp. 390 f. (Lecture II,
n.18); and note that of recent years the view has been revived that the form
should be taken in a passive sense. Cf. H. Torczyner, *Z.D.M.G.* lxxxv (1931),
p. 322, who thinks that it denoted one who was 'possessed' or perhaps
originally one who had been 'called' by the Spirit; Jepsen, op. cit., p. 10, who
takes it to mean 'der Erregte, der berufene Bote', on the assumption that
'erregen' is the original meaning of the root; Guillaume, op. cit., pp. 112 f.,
where it is argued that linguistically the word denotes 'one who is in the
state of announcing a message which has been given to him'; Albright,
From the Stone Age to Christianity (1957 edit.), p. 303, who stresses the
Accadian connexion and maintains that it denotes one who has been 'called'
by God to communicate the divine will: and, similarly, A. Haldar, *Associations of Cult Prophets among the Ancient Semites* (1945), p. 109, n. 2; Buber,
loc. cit. (i.e. as a view which merits consideration); J. Lindblom, 'Zur Frage
des kanaanäischen Ursprungs des alttestamentlichen Prophetismus', in *Von
Ugarit nach Qumran* (O. Eissfeldt *Festschrift*), ed. J. Hempel and L. Rost,
B.Z.A.W. 77 (1958), p. 102; D. W. Thomas, 'Again "The Prophet" in
the Lachish Ostraca', ibid., p. 249, n. 23; and R. Rendtorff, *Th.W.N.T.* vi
(1959), p. 796. See also, for a brief general discussion of the question, Rowley,
op. cit., pp. 97 f.; and, for a comparatively full survey of the conflict of
opinion prior to the year 1926, van den Oudenrijn, op. cit., pp. 26 ff.

[1] e.g. 1 Kings xiv. 1 ff. (as above, p. 23).
[2] e.g. 2 Kings iii. 6 ff. (as above, pp. 19 f.). Cf. the interesting discussion
by Thomas, op. cit., of the passing reference to 'the prophet' in Lachish
Letter III.

attend; in short, there were specially sacred times and places for such consultation. This is borne out, in the first place, by the fact that, when the Shunammite woman wished to seek the aid of Elisha in restoring her child to life, her husband said to her:[1]

Why dost thou go to him today? It is neither New Moon nor Sabbath.

Such an obviously cultic association, coupled with the fact that Elisha was to be visited at Mount Carmel, the site of an early and famous sanctuary, is sufficient of itself to prove that the prophet had a connexion of some sort with the formal worship of Yahweh;[2] but, what is more, such a connexion may be traced from the very beginning. Thus even in the story of the seventy elders it is only after they have been stationed around the sacred tent that they begin to 'act the נָבִיא'.[3] Similarly the נְבִיאִים whom Saul finds acting so characteristically are on their way down from the 'high place' at Gibeah.[4] Further it is said of Samuel that he was permanently established as a prophet at the important sanctuary of Shiloh, where his prophetic 'word' was never spoken without effect.[5] Again, it was a prophet, i.e. Nathan,

---

[1] 2 Kings iv. 23.

[2] Cf. verses 25 ff.; and see below, p. 27, n. 4.

[3] Num. xi. 24b–30 (E). It is thought that this story may reflect later conditions in Canaan. Cf., for example, B. Baentsch, H.K. (1903), and H. Holzinger, K.H.C. (1903), *in loc.*; T. H. Robinson, *Prophecy and the Prophets in Ancient Israel*, p. 34; Lindblom, op. cit., pp. 99 ff.

[4] 1 Sam. x. 5, 10: cf. R.V. mgn., R.S.V.

[5] 1 Sam. iii, esp. 19–21: see below, pp. 36 ff. Another famous prophet is said to have been stationed at Shiloh a century or so later; for it was to Shiloh that Jeroboam I sent his wife that she might consult Ahijah concerning their son's illness. See above, p. 23, n. 8, p. 25, n. 1: and, with further reference to Ahijah, 1 Kings xi. 29 ff., xii. 15 (cf. 2 Chron. x. 15), xv. 29; 2 Chron. ix. 29. Of course it is usually held that the temple at Shiloh was destroyed at the time of the Philistine invasion recorded in 1 Sam. iv, although there is no direct statement to this effect in the passage mentioned. Cf., for example, R. Kittel, op. cit., p. 72; E. Sellin, *Geschichte des israelitisch-jüdischen Volkes*, i (1924), p. 143; W. O. E. Oesterley and T. H. Robinson, *A History of Israel* (1932), i, p. 163; M. Noth, *Geschichte Israels*, 3rd edit. rev. (1956), pp. 92 f., 154, E.T., 2nd edit. rev. by P. R. Ackroyd, *The History of Israel* (1960), pp. 95 f., 166 f.; J. Bright, *A History of Israel* (1960), p. 165: and, for the archaeo-

whom David apparently first consulted concerning his pro-
ject for a sanctuary in Jerusalem; and thereupon it was
through Nathan's prophetic 'word' or 'observation', we are
told, that the building of Solomon's Temple was fore-
shadowed.[1] Moreover, it is highly suggestive that it should
have been Nathan, a prophet, and Zadok, a priest, who co-
operated (but with the former as the principal agent) in
having Solomon anointed as king.[2] The most valuable evidence, however, is again furnished by the stories which
centre in the persons of Elijah and Elisha; for, whatever
their immediate historical value,[3] they may safely be regarded as presenting a true picture of the typical נָבִיא. Thus
it is significant to find that, when Elijah, as Yahweh's sole
surviving protagonist among the prophets, threw down his
famous challenge to the prophets of the Tyrian Baal, he
staged a sacrificial scene at one of the many sanctuaries
where Yahweh's altar had been reduced to ruin.[4] Moreover,
it is not to be assumed that this close connexion between
prophet and altar was something abnormal; for, when
Elijah thereupon fled from Mount Carmel to Horeb, and
Yahweh asked him what he was doing so far south, he

---

logical evidence now adduced in support of this view, H. Kjaer, 'The Excava-
tion of Shiloh 1929', *J.P.O.S.* x (1930), pp. 87–174, esp. 91–109; *I det hellige
land. De Danske udgravninger i Shilo, Elis' og Samuels' by* (1931), esp.
pp. 28 ff. See, however, S. A. Cook, *The Old Testament: A Reinterpretation*
(1936), pp. 53 f.; and note that, even if this be so, it need not imply that
all the cultic associations of so important a sacred site came to an end—
any more than was the case after the destruction of Solomon's Temple at
Jerusalem in 587 B.C. Cf., for example, Oesterley and Robinson, op. cit. ii,
pp. 91 ff.

[1] 2 Sam. vii. 1 ff.; 1 Chron. xvii. 1 ff. See above, p. 13, n. 3.

[2] 1 Kings i. It should be borne in mind, however, that inasmuch as the
term נָבִיא received an extension in meaning, it may well be that Nathan, like
Gad, was not a נָבִיא of the early type but rather a חֹזֶה or 'seer'. See above,
pp. 15 f.; also 1 Sam. xxii. 5. Similarly the above-mentioned conception of
Samuel's cultic role at Shiloh may be based upon the figure of a חֹזֶה rather
than that of the early type of 'prophet'.

[3] See further, for example, among the works cited above, p. 1, n. 1:
Eissfeldt, pp. 349 ff.; Oesterley and Robinson, pp. 98 ff.; Pfeiffer, pp. 403 ff.;
Bentzen, i, pp. 237 ff.

[4] 1 Kings xviii. Note verse 30; and cf. xix. 10 (as quoted below in the
text). See also F.-M. Abel, *Géographie de la Palestine*, i (1933), p. 351.

coupled altar and prophet together in the following remarkable way:[1]

> I have been very jealous for Yahweh, the God of Hosts, because the children of Israel have forsaken Thy covenant, demolished Thine altars, and slain Thy prophets with the sword; I alone am left, and they seek my life to take it away.

These words recall the incident of the hundred prophets whom Obadiah saved from the murderous intent of Jezebel;[2] and, in the circumstances, there seems no reason to doubt that the whole reflects a rivalry between two different cults and their respective specialists,[3] i.e. those of the Tyrian Baal on the one side and those of Yahweh on the other. This rivalry reached its climax, of course, in the days of Elisha who, like Elijah, is represented as having connexions with the sanctuary on Mount Carmel;[4] for, when Jehu (at the instigation of Elisha) secured the throne of the Northern Kingdom, he promptly made a clean sweep of the foreign cult. The way in which he issued his subtle instructions for the slaughter is to be noted. Thus he says:[5]

> Ahab served the Baal a little; Jehu will serve him much. Now therefore call unto me all the prophets of the Baal (all his worshippers) and all his priests; let none be wanting, for I have a great sacrifice for the Baal. . . .

This passage only confirms what is already made obvious by the story of Elijah's contest with the prophets of the Baal. The latter are clearly attached to the cultus of a god of high, if not the highest, rank;[6] they form a part (and,

---

[1] 1 Kings xix. 10: cf. 14. Note, too, that Balaam's oracular utterances were accompanied by sacrificial rites: Num. xxiii. 1 ff., 14 ff., 29 f. (JE). It has been suggested, moreover, that the hairy mantle, which was typical of at least a certain class of prophet, was the skin of some sacrificial victim; as such it might have been thought to afford means of entering more closely into communion with one's God. The potent mantle which Elisha is said to have inherited from Elijah may be regarded in this light. Cf. 1 Kings xix. 13, 19; 2 Kings i. 8, ii. 8, 13 f.; Zech. xiii. 4: and see further Hölscher, op. cit., pp. 145 f. It must be said, however, that the present writer is far from being convinced that this was the case.   [2] 1 Kings xviii. 4.

[3] One might well say 'agents': see below, pp. 36 ff.

[4] See above, pp. 25 f.   [5] 2 Kings x. 18 f.

[6] Cf. O. Eissfeldt, *R.G.G.*[3] i (1957), art. 'Baal'.

indeed, what looks like the leading or most important part)[1] of the cultic personnel. They are certainly not to be regarded as individuals working independently in an unattached sort of way. Accordingly it seems only reasonable to infer that their rivals held a similar position in the cultus of Yahweh, and, in doing so, had links of either a permanent or an occasional character with different sanctuaries throughout the country.[2]

III

The preceding evidence, however, is far from being all which may be cited in support of the view that, in point of time at least, the part played by the prophet in the drama of Israelite religion was primarily that of a cultic specialist.[3]

---

[1] See below, pp. 62 ff.

[2] e.g. in addition to those mentioned in the text: at Bethel (2 Kings ii. 3), Gilgal (iv. 38 ff.; cf. ii. 1), and Jericho (ii. 5). See further Hölscher, op. cit., pp. 143 ff.; also *Geschichte der israelitischen und jüdischen Religion* (1922), pp. 83 ff. As the stories stand, Elisha seems to have been associated for some time with the important sanctuary on Mount Carmel—and, perhaps, with such another in Samaria, which was the capital city of the Northern Kingdom. Cf. 2 Kings iv. 1–37, v ff.; also ii. 25. Moreover, despite the legendary character of some of these stories, it may well be that the prophets (at least in the Northern Kingdom) were united under the leadership of one of their number with his headquarters at some particularly influential cultic centre. The frequent intercourse thus involved would account for the apparent itineraries of both Elijah and Elisha. Cf. esp. 2 Kings ii and iv. For valuable comparative data at this point, see the account of the part played by the Islamic brotherhoods of North Africa at the shrines of the various welis or 'saints', as described by Dermenghem, loc. cit.; and note in this connexion the argument of W. F. Albright, 'The High Place in Ancient Palestine', in *Volume du Congrès: Strasbourg 1956*, S.V.T. iv (1957), pp. 242–58, to the effect that in some cases the בָּמָה, qua 'high place', was originally a mortuary shrine. Cf., too, Pedersen, 'The Rôle played by Inspired Persons among the Israelites and the Arabs' (as cited above, p. 4, n. 7), pp. 130 ff.

[3] In view of the comments made by Eichrodt, loc. cit., and indeed the earlier comment made by N. W. Porteous, 'Living Issues in Biblical Scholarship: Prophet and Priest in Israel', *E.T.* lxii (1950–1), p. 7, n. 9, it may be as well to point out that in the present writer's opinion and despite what appears to be the simple equation of 'cult' and 'worship' in, say, *S.O.E.D.*, s.v., the former term is really more embracing than the latter. Cf., for example, W. B. Selbie, *The Psychology of Religion* (1924), cor. imp. (1926), chap. v, 'Cult and Worship': S. Mowinckel, *Religion und Kultus* (1953), *passim*;

The fact is that, as the foregoing pages have served to show, a right appreciation of the prophetic role can be secured only by considering evidence which goes far beyond the figures of the canonical prophets. The latter are apt to be studied apart from the general background of prophetic activity in their own time; and, as a result of the protests which some of them make against sacrifice for example,[1] this has led to a totally misleading picture of the typical prophet as an individual who tends to oppose all cultic forms.[2] Indeed, much of the material for a true appreciation of the prophetic role is provided by certain of the canonical prophets themselves in their polemic against contemporary נְבִיאִים; and, taken as a whole, it gives a colourful picture both of their consultative capacity and of their association with the cultus—particularly that of the Jerusalem Temple. At the same time it must be borne in mind that, owing to the wider extension of the term נָבִיא,[3] it is impossible to say how far the prophets under discussion were characterized by the behaviour typical of the early נְבִיאִים. The functions of the רֹאֶה or חֹזֶה and the early נָבִיא obviously overlapped; and this must account for the fact that eventually the last term largely supplanted the first two.

Now it is to be observed from the outset that the above-mentioned polemic is directed, not against the actual function of the prophets concerned, but against the abuse of

---

R.G.G.[3] iv (1960), art. 'Kultus'. That is to say, the term 'cult' (*or* 'cultus') may be and, indeed, should be used to include all those religious exercises which form the established means employed by any social group for (*a*) securing right relations with the realm of what is 'sacred' or 'holy', and (*b*) thus enjoying those benefits, including guidance in the various crises of life, which this realm is thought capable of bestowing upon mankind.

[1] e.g. Isa. i. 11 ff.; Jer. vii. 21 ff.; Hos. vi. 6; Amos v. 21 ff.; Mic. vi. 6 ff.

[2] It is interesting to note that strong criticism of such a picture appeared in a work which was published at about the same time as the writer's original article, 'The Prophet in Israelite Worship' (see above, p. vi): i.e. A. C. Welch, *Prophet and Priest in Old Israel* (1936). The caution with which this whole question needs to be approached has now rightly been stressed in much fuller terms by H. H. Rowley, 'The Unity of the Old Testament', *B.J.R.L.* xxix (1945–6), pp. 326 ff., *The Unity of the Bible* (1953), pp. 30 ff.

[3] See above, pp. 9 ff.

their office and the falsity of their oracles.[1] Micah, for
example, denounces his contemporaries in the following
terms:[2]

> Thus saith Yahweh concerning the prophets
> Who are leading My people astray,
> Who munch away with their teeth
> And keep proclaiming 'Peace!';
> But if anyone doth not put into their mouth,
> Against him they start a war.
> Therefore it shall be night for you without חָזוֹן,
> And darkness for you without קֶסֶם;
> The sun shall go down upon the prophets,
> And over them the day shall grow dark.

Here it is perfectly clear that the prophets are being condemned, not for their function as such, but because they
are abusing their office for mercenary ends—giving oracles
or promises of 'Peace (שָׁלוֹם)!'[3] to those who pay them sufficiently well but stirring up trouble for those who fail to
satisfy their greed.[4]

Moreover, it is highly significant that, whether or not this
be true of the seer or the early type of prophet, קֶסֶם is here
a recognized part of the prophetic function; for it adds emphasis to the fact that the prophets were consulted for the
sake of their peculiar powers. The general meaning of the
term קֶסֶם is beyond dispute, for in Arabic the cognate verbal

---

[1] This means that one must be on one's guard against easy generalizations
with regard to 'false' and 'true' prophets; and, happily, the complexity of this
question is now being increasingly recognized. Cf., for example, K. Harms,
Die falschen Propheten (1947); G. Quell, *Wahre und falsche Propheten*,
B.F.C.T. 46. 1 (1952); E. Jacob, 'Quelques remarques sur les faux prophètes',
T.Z. xiii (1957), pp. 479–86; Rendtorff, op. cit., pp. 806 ff.: also Rowley,
B.J.R.L. xxix (1945–6), pp. 331 f., *The Unity of the Bible*, p. 37, and 'Ritual
and the Hebrew Prophets' (as cited above, p. 2, n. 1), pp. 247 ff.

[2] iii. 5 f. In verse 6 the form קֹסֵם may be repointed as קֶסֶם without change
of meaning.

[3] See below, pp. 49 ff.

[4] The reference seems to be to an abuse of privilege, inasmuch as it was
apparently customary for both the seer and the early type of prophet to
receive a gift of some kind in return for services rendered. Cf. 1 Sam. ix. 7 f.;
1 Kings xiv. 3; also 2 Kings v, *passim*, viii. 8 f.: and see further Smith and
Irwin, op. cit., pp. 8 ff.

form قَسَمَ was used at one time (in conjugation X) with reference to a special type of sacred lot, i.e. that in which a number of headless arrows, each representing one of the several possibilities in mind, would be placed in a quiver and whirled about, and the first to be drawn out was then taken to represent the divine decision.[1] Indeed Ezekiel has drawn a notable picture of Nebuchadnezzar's resorting to what appears to be just such a device;[2] but, even so, this seems to be represented[3] as but one of three forms of קֶסֶם, the others being the consultation of תְּרָפִים[4] and the examina-

---

[1] Cf. W. R. Smith, *J.P.* xiii (1885), pp. 276 ff.; J. Wellhausen, *Reste arabischen Heidentums*, 2nd edit. (1897), pp. 132 f.: also Dhorme, *R.H.R.* cviii (1933), pp. 119 f., *L'Évolution religieuse d'Israël. I: La Religion des Hébreux nomades*, pp. 227 ff.   [2] xxi. 26 f. (EVV. 21 f.).

[3] Contrary to the view of both Smith and Wellhausen, loc. cit.

[4] The literature on the תְּרָפִים is extensive, as may be seen from the relevant articles in such standard works of reference as *E.B.* (G. F. Moore), *D.B.* (A. C. Welch), *E.R.E.* (A. Lods). The term itself is found only in the plural, at least so far as the Old Testament is concerned, unless this plural form is to be explained in some cases, if not in all, as being due to a misunderstanding of what was originally a singular noun with mimation. Cf. A. Jirku, *Biblica* xxxiv (1953), pp. 78–80, who would explain the terms אוּרִים and תֻּמִּים (as discussed above, p. 6, n. 2) in the same way. The etymology of the word and its meaning are similarly matters of dispute. So far as its derivation is concerned, opinion now seems most divided over a suggested connexion with: (a) The Hebrew רְפָאִים (as denoting the shades of the dead). On this theory the objects in question may be associated with ancestor worship. Cf., for example, F. Schwally, *Das Leben nach dem Tode* (1892), pp. 35 ff.; W. O. E. Oesterley and T. H. Robinson, *Hebrew Religion*, 2nd edit. rev. (1937), pp. 100 f.; R. Brinker, *The Influence of Sanctuaries in Early Israel* (1946), pp. 62–64. (b) The so-called New (or Late) Hebrew תֹּרֶף (as denoting 'filth, rottenness, decay'). On this theory the term may have a quite general reference to sundry objectionable objects as 'rotten (*or* filthy) things'. Cf. now, for example, Lods, *Israël*, p. 500, E.T., p. 431; Albright, *From the Stone Age to Christianity*, p. 311; P. R. Ackroyd, 'The Teraphim', *E.T.* lxii (1950–1), pp. 378–80. Further, it has been thought that, despite its plural form (and like the term אֱלֹהִים, as used of 'God', a 'god', or 'gods'), it may refer equally well to one or more than one object: cf. (a) 1 Sam. xix. 13, 16; (b) Gen. xxxi. 34 (E), and note again Jirku's theory of mimation as referred to above. Moreover the former passage is commonly read as indicating that Michal could place one in David's bed and arrange it in such a way as to suggest his figure; and this has led some scholars to suppose that in form and size it was like a man, or, at least, that it was so in certain cases. Cf., for example, H. Gunkel, *H.K.*, 3rd edit. rev. (1910), and J. Skinner, *I.C.C.* (1910), on Gen. xxxi. 19 (E); P. (E.) Dhorme, *E.B.* (1910), on 1 Sam. xix. 13; H. H. Rowley, *B.J.R.L.* xxxiv (1951–2), pp. 103 f. Others find it difficult to reconcile this with the

tion of the liver of a sacrificial victim.¹ Moreover, consultation of the dead² and the interpretation of dreams³ were
also included under this head; so that the term must have
had quite a general application as denoting various forms of

statement that Rachel hid two or more by placing them in the saddle-basket
of a camel and sitting upon them. Cf., for example, C. F. Burney, *The Book
of Judges*, 2nd edit. (1920), p. 420, with reference to Gen. xxxi. 34. Accordingly it has been suggested, on the one hand, that the object in question may
have been an image in the shape of a head or bust; and the fact that it was
used for purposes of consultation has also given rise to the theory that it
was a kind of mantic mask. Cf., for example, H. Ewald, *Die Alterthümer des
Volkes Israel = Geschichte des Volkes Israel, Anhang zum zweiten und dritten
Bande*, 3rd edit. rev. (1866), pp. 296 ff., E.T. by H. S. Solly, *The Antiquities
of Israel* (1876), pp. 223 ff.; H. Gressmann, *Mose und seine Zeit* (1913), pp. 249
and 452; A. Jirku, *Mantik in Altisrael* (1913), pp. 13–28; J. Herrmann,
K.A.T. (1924), on Ezek. xxi. 26 (EVV. 21); Brinker, loc. cit. In illustration
of such cultic masks see now the recent discoveries at Canaanite Hazor, as
described by Y. Yadin (and others), *Hazor I: An Account of the First Season of
Excavations, 1955* (1958), p. 138 and pl. clxiii, and esp. *Hazor II: An Account
of the Second Season of Excavations, 1956* (1960), p. 115 and pls. clxxxii and
clxxxiii. Note, however, Hänel, op. cit., p. 245, n. 1: also the fact that Gressmann subsequently rejected the theory of a mantic mask in favour of a
medium-sized image in human form, the head of which could be manipu-
lated when the object was consulted; and the etymology was then explained
in terms of *רָפַף√תֶּרֶף, 'to move to and fro, quiver, tremble'. Cf. S.A.T.
ii. 1, 2nd edit. rev. (1921), p. 81, and esp. G. Hoffmann and H. Gressmann,
'Teraphim, Masken und Winkorakel in Ägypten und Vorderasien', *Z.A.W.*
xl (1922), pp. 75–137. Alternatively it is suggested that the above-mentioned
interpretation of 1 Sam. xix. 13 and 16 is due to a mistranslation of the
Hebrew, which points to the תְּרָפִים as being placed *by* (not *in*) David's bed;
and that accordingly the term should be taken here, too, in a plural sense as
having reference, not to a life-size figure or even a head or bust, but to
prophylactic figurines of the terra-cotta type now recovered in considerable
numbers from sites in Palestine and the Near East generally. Cf. W. E.
Barnes, 'Teraphim', *J.T.S.* xxx (1928–9), pp. 177–9; and S. Smith, 'What
were the Teraphim?', *J.T.S.* xxxiii (1931–2), pp. 33–36, who would then
derive the term from √רפא, 'to heal', as denoting 'those who bring health'.
See also W. C. Graham and H. G. May, *Culture and Conscience* (1936),
pp. 93 f., and Albright, loc. cit., where the view is advanced that the term
was used in a general sense to include figurines of the mother-goddess type.
Finally, for the possible use of black and white figurines in divination, see
C. J. Gadd, *Ideas of Divine Rule in the Ancient East* (1948), p. 95.
  ¹ Cf. G. Contenau, *La Médecine en Assyrie et en Babylonie* (1938), pp. 105–
22, *La Divination chez les Assyriens et les Babyloniens* (1940), pp. 235–69;
and, in illustration of a clay model of an animal's liver, inscribed with omens,
which was found in the ruins of Temple II at Hazor (cf. the previous note),
Y. Yadin, 'The Fourth Season of Excavations at Hazor', *B.A.* xxii (1959),
pp. 7 f.   ² Cf. 1 Sam. xxviii. 8.   ³ Cf. Zech. x. 2.

inquiry concerning the future, and is well represented by the usual English rendering 'divination'.[1] Finally, the wisdom literature has preserved interesting testimony to the value placed upon 'divination'; for it records the proverbial saying:[2]

> There is divination on the lips of a king;
> His mouth is not treacherous in judgement.

In other words, the king's ruling upon any matter is as trustworthy as one secured by means of קֶסֶם or 'divination'; and this may be the more readily understood, if one pauses to consider the role of the Davidic king as Yahweh's vice-gerent to whom all difficult cases might be referred.[3] Accordingly, although the exact forms of divination practised by the prophets may be uncertain, one thing is clear: during the monarchical period, at least, it was recognized as an authoritative branch of the prophetic activity. If more decisive evidence be sought, it may be found in Micah's general denunciation of certain outstanding figures in Jerusalem:[4]

> Her leaders pass judgement for a bribe,
> And her priests give direction at a price,
> And her prophets divine for money;
> Yet it is upon Yahweh that they lean, saying,
> 'Is not Yahweh in our midst?
> No evil can come upon us!'

Here קֶסֶם is placed upon the same plane as the judgement of a civic leader and the direction of a priest;[5] it is recognized (by a canonical prophet, be it noted) as a valid method of securing a decision in the affairs of life. The prophets, like the other officials, are condemned, not for the exercise of what is clearly regarded as their normal function, but for its abuse.[6] Hence once again it is obvious that 'divination' was an authoritative form of the prophetic activity;

---

[1] Cf. M. Gaster, *E.R.E.*, art. 'Divination (Jewish)'.
[2] Prov. xvi. 10.
[3] Cf. *Sacral Kingship in Ancient Israel*, pp. 3 ff., 106, n. 5.
[4] iii. 11.   [5] See above, pp. 4 ff.   [6] See above, p. 31, n. 4.

and still further confirmation of this may be found in the fact that the prophets evidently claim, in common with the other consultative specialists, that they enjoy Yahweh's support.[1]

It is to be observed, however, that this oracular guidance might be secured, not only by means of קֶסֶם or 'divination', but also through the medium of a חָזוֹן or, as this term is usually rendered, a 'vision'. This appears readily enough in the first part of Micah iii. 5–7, quoted above,[2] where the prophets in the case are condemned for returning favourable

---

[1] The exact significance of two well-known passages, which appear to suggest that קֶסֶם or 'divination' is something foreign to the true Israel, is, in each case, a matter of dispute. Thus (i) it is commonly thought that in Num. xxiii. 23 (JE) we have a statement to the effect that there is no קֶסֶם *in* Israel (cf. A.V. mgn., R.V.); and, as a result, the verse as a whole is found to have so little bearing on the context that it is frequently regarded as an interpolation. Cf., for example, G. B. Gray, I.C.C. (1912), *in loc.* It is by no means certain, however, that the passage should be taken in this way. In fact it seems much more likely that the preposition in question should be construed as meaning, not 'in', but 'against' (cf. A.V., R.V. mgn., R.S.V.); for this yields a meaning in complete harmony with the context, the point being that Balaam is unable to curse the Israelites, because he knows that the future holds nothing ominous *against* Israel. Again (ii) in Deut. xviii. 9–22 an attempt is made to define the role of the true נָבִיא, who is contrasted sharply with (*a*) the קֹסֵם or 'diviner', and (*b*) several other types of individual, all of whom make corresponding but illegitimate claims to determine the future, e.g. the kind of necromancer associated with the term אוֹב: A.V. 'a consulter with familiar spirits', R.V. 'a consulter with a familiar spirit', R.S.V. 'a medium'. As we have seen, however, the root under discussion (קָסַם, 'divination'; קָסַם, 'to divine') could itself be used with reference to different means of determining the future *including* the form of necromancy associated with the term אוֹב. See above, pp. 31 ff., especially the citation of 1 Sam. xxviii. 8: A.V. 'I pray thee, divine unto me by the familiar spirit', R.V. 'Divine unto me, I pray thee, by the familiar spirit', R.S.V. 'Divine for me by a spirit'. This suggests that the root in question could be used in both a narrow and a broad sense. Accordingly it may well be that a נָבִיא could be described as a קֹסֵם, *qua* one who had the means of determining the future, without his thereby being equated with the קֹסֵם *qua* one who did so in a particular (and, for the author of Deut. xviii. 9–22, an offensive) way. After all (as we have seen above, pp. 9 ff.), the term נָבִיא could be used of markedly different types of 'prophet'; and, what is more, one of these types is condemned in Zech. xiii. 1–6, *qua* נָבִיא, in terms as specific as those used in Deut. xviii. 9–22 with reference to the קֹסֵם! The fact is that here again, as indeed so often, we must be on our guard against over-simplifying the issue: cf. p. 22, n. 3, p. 31, n. 1.

[2] See p. 31.

oracles (the alleged outcome of 'vision' and 'divination') to those who pay them sufficiently well. The matter is placed beyond dispute, however, by the latter part of the passage:[1]

> Yea, they that have 'visions' will be shamefaced,
> And they that practise 'divination' will blush;
> And they will all of them cover their lips
> Through there being no answer from God.

Altogether these lines offer further proof of the fact that 'visions', like 'divination', formed a recognized method of securing divine guidance in response to definite inquiry, and that, therefore, they might be secured as occasion demanded; whatever their practice, the prophets were consulted for the sake of their oracular powers.[2]

The term חָזוֹן, however, must not be taken too literally as having constant reference to a strictly visual or even an auditory experience.[3] Such parallelism as the above[4] suggests that it could be used as a synonym for קֶסֶם; and, indeed, this appears to be confirmed by the fact that the verbal form from √חזה is found in conjunction with the term קֶסֶם to denote what seems best rendered as the 'observation' of the latter.[5] Accordingly Micah's words, as translated above, should probably be rendered thus:

> Yea, they that 'observe' will be shamefaced,
> And they that 'divine' will blush;
> And they will all of them cover their lips
> Through there being no answer from God.

Or again:

> Yea, they that 'make observations' will be shamefaced,
> And they that 'practise divination' will blush;
> &c.

---

[1] N.B. 'they that have "visions"' (הַחֹזִים) corresponds to 'the seers' of EVV. and R.S.V., while 'they that practise "divination"' (הַקֹּסְמִים) corresponds to 'the diviners' of EVV. and R.S.V.; but the reader should relate the parallelism of this line to the corresponding parallelism of verse 6a, as quoted above, p. 31.   [2] See further Ezek. xiv. 7 ff.   [3] See above, pp. 12 ff.

[4] Cf. Jer. xiv. 13 f., as below, pp. 50 f.; Ezek. xiii. 6 ff., as below, p. 52 (in part), xiii. 23, xxi. 34 (EVV. 29), xxii. 28, as below, p. 52.

[5] Ezek. xiii. 6, as below, p. 52. Cf. Zech. x. 2: 'The "diviners" have "observed" falsely.'

This is quite in keeping with the fact that, as already noted, when חָזוֹן is used in connexion with the prophetic activity, it is more or less synonymous with דָּבָר or 'word', and may be rendered more suitably by 'observation'.[1] Thus one learns that, just as advice was to be expected of the elders or the wise, and just as direction might be secured from the priest, so a חָזוֹן or דָּבָר, an 'observation' or 'word', might be sought (and again one may note the statement that the חָזוֹן might be sought) from the prophet.[2] Moreover, without prejudice as to the general question of any connexion between the canonical prophets and the cultus,[3] one may note that Ezekiel supplies two excellent illustrations of the close practical affinity between these two terms when he says:[4]

The 'Word' of Yahweh came unto me saying: Son of man, what is this proverb that ye have throughout the land of Israel, saying, 'The days lengthen, and every "observation" (חָזוֹן) cometh to nought'? Therefore say unto them: 'Thus saith the Lord Yahweh! I am putting an end to this proverb, and it shall be used no more in Israel.' In fact, say unto them: 'The days are at hand—and the דָּבָר of every "observation" (חָזוֹן). . . .'

The 'Word' of Yahweh came unto me saying: Son of man, lo, the house of Israel are saying, 'The "observation" (חָזוֹן) which he doth make (*lit.* "observe") is for many days to come, and it is of distant times that he doth prophesy.' Therefore say unto them: 'Thus saith the Lord Yahweh! None of My "Words" (דְּבָרִים) shall drag on any more. When I speak a "Word" (דָּבָר), it shall be performed.'
Oracle of the Lord Yahweh!

Here it is clear that the 'word' which the prophet utters as his 'observation' is the very 'Word' of Yahweh, and, as such, has something of an objective reality. When Yahweh says a 'thing', it is done; the spoken 'word' (דָּבָר) is actually

---

[1] See above, pp. 12 ff.
[2] Jer. xviii. 18; Ezek. vii. 26: see above, p. 7.
[3] See below, pp. 64 f.
[4] xii. 21–28.

one with the 'thing' (דָּבָר) which is to be 'performed'.[1] This is made obvious by the announcement:[2]

> The days are at hand—
> and the דָּבָר[3] of every חָזוֹן.[4]

Indeed the whole idea is summed up in a charming passage from a writer who was almost contemporary with Ezekiel. Speaking on behalf of Yahweh he says:[5]

> As the rain and the snow
>   Come down from heaven,
> And return not thither,
>   But water the earth
> And make it bring forth and bud,
>   That it may give seed to the sower and bread to the eater,
> So shall My 'Word' be that goeth forth out of My Mouth;
>   It shall not return unto Me void,
> But it shall perform that which I please,
>   And succeed in that whereto I sent it.

These well-known lines (which also illustrate, once again, the significance attached to the prophetic 'word' in its relation to Yahweh)[6] clearly reflect that primitive and widespread conception of the power of the spoken word which

---

[1] For a discussion of the term דָּבָר, as denoting both 'word' and 'thing', see O. Grether, *Name und Wort Gottes im Alten Testament*, B.Z.A.W. 64 (1934), pp. 59 ff.; and, as representing the content or subject-'matter' of a vision, pp. 97 ff.; and finally, on being powerful in its own right as a prophetic utterance, pp. 103 ff.

[2] Some editors would read a verbal form instead of דָּבָר, thereby securing a parallel to the syntax of the fore-mentioned proverb. Cf., for example, Herrmann, op. cit., and G. Fohrer, H.A.T. (1955), *in loc.* Such a suggestion, however, besides being somewhat artificial, misses the significance of the term דָּבָר; and the M.T. is rightly retained by G. A. Cooke, I.C.C. (1936), as also by the translators of R.S.V.

[3] EVV.: 'effect', R.S.V.: 'fulfilment'.   [4] EVV., R.S.V.: 'vision'.

[5] Isa. lv. 10 f.: cf. Isa. ix. 7 (EVV. 8); Jer. i. 11 f.; and esp. 1 Sam. iii. 11, i.e. 'Yahweh said to Samuel: Lo, I am performing a דָּבָר in Israel at which both ears of everyone that heareth it shall tingle.' Here again דָּבָר has a double significance, according as the emphasis falls upon the 'thing' which is to be performed or the 'word' which shall be heard. When the prophetic 'word' proved effectual, it was said to have been set up; but if it turned out to be ineffectual, it was said to have fallen to the ground. Cf. 1 Sam. iii. 19; 1 Kings xii. 15; Ezek. xiii. 6, as below, p. 52.

[6] See further *The One and the Many in the Israelite Conception of God*,

lies behind so many magical practices; and there is good
reason to believe that, so far as the prophets in general
were concerned, this conception was often something more
than mere poetical imagery. In fact, it is wholly in line with
those magical ideas which have been rightly recognized as
lying behind their so-called symbolism.[1]

Thus, when Ahab sought the דָּבָר or 'Word' of Yahweh,
and the four hundred or so prophets carried out the usual
exercises to this end, their leader Zedekiah made or, rather,
produced[2] a pair of iron horns, and said:[3]

pp. 20 f., 2nd edit., p. 17, where the writer has attempted to show that the
prophetic 'word', as being the very 'Word' of Yahweh, forms one of those
important 'Extensions' of Yahweh's Personality which anticipate the so-
called 'Hypostases' of later Judaism. Cf. W. Bousset, *Die Religion des Juden-
tums im späthellenistischen Zeitalter*, 3rd edit. rev. by H. Gressmann (1926),
pp. 342 ff., S. Mowinckel, *R.G.G.*[2] ii (1928), and H. Ringgren, *R.G.G.*[3] iii
(1959), art. 'Hypostasen'; and, in illustration of the consequent need to
investigate the whole problem afresh, G. F. Moore, *Judaism in the First
Centuries of the Christian Era: The Age of the Tannaim*, i (1927), pp. 414 ff.
See also, for further discussion of the term under consideration, J. Szeruda,
Das Wort Jahwes (1921), L. Dürr, *Die Wertung des göttlichen Wortes im Alten
Testament und im antiken Orient* (1938), O. Procksch, *Th.W.N.T.* iv (1942),
pp. 89 ff.; also T. Boman, *Das hebräische Denken im Vergleich mit dem
Griechischen*, 3rd edit. rev. (1959), pp. 45–53, E.T. by J. L. Moreau, *Hebrew
Thought compared with Greek* (1960), pp. 58–67.

[1] The ultimate significance of such prophetic symbolism, as compared
with its magical background, remains to be determined, although some valuable work on the subject has been done in recent years. See especially (*a*)
H. W. Robinson, 'Prophetic Symbolism', in the symposium *Old Testament
Essays*, with a foreword by D. C. Simpson (1927), pp. 1–17, 'Hebrew Sacrifice and Prophetic Symbolism', *J.T.S.* xliii (1941–2), pp. 129–39; and, for
the argument in a wider setting, *Redemption and Revelation* (1942), pp. xxxi f.,
106, 155 f., 250 f., *Inspiration and Revelation in the Old Testament* (1946),
pp. 35 f., 185 f., 226 ff., and *Two Hebrew Prophets* (1948), pp. 84 ff.: (*b*) A.
van den Born, *Profetie Metterdaad: Een studie over de symbolische handelingen
der profeten* (1947): (*c*) G. Fohrer, 'Die Gattung der Berichte über symbolische Handlungen der Propheten', *Z.A.W.* lxiv (1952), pp. 101–20, *Die
symbolischen Handlungen der Propheten*, A.T.A.N.T. 25 (1953): also (*d*) Guillaume, op. cit., pp. 169 ff.; C. A. Keller, *Das Wort OTH als 'Offenbarungszeichen Gottes'* (1946), as cited below, p. 53, n. 2.

[2] Cf. Guillaume, op. cit., p. 145, n. 2, who reminds one that the horns
may have been a 'cult object': and, for the governing motif, see Hölscher,
Die Profeten, p. 146, n. 4, *Geschichte der israelitischen und jüdischen Religion*,
§ 34, n. 18; G. Widengren, *The Accadian and Hebrew Psalms of Lamentation
as Religious Documents* (1937), pp. 255 f.

[3] 1 Kings xxii. 11; 2 Chron. xviii. 10.

Thus saith Yahweh!
With these shalt thou gore the Aramaeans
—*completely*!

In so doing Zedekiah was attempting to create victory for
Ahab, just as Elisha later used a similar method to secure
Joash's triumph over these hereditary enemies of Israel. On
this occasion Elisha, with his hands laid upon those of the
king, bade the latter shoot an arrow through the window on
the east side of the room, and said in explanation and en-
forcement of the act:[1]

> An arrow of victory for Yahweh,
> An arrow of victory over the Aramaeans!
> So shalt thou smite the Aramaeans in Aphek
> —*completely*!

Moreover, in the concluding scene the king incurs Elisha's
displeasure by smiting upon the ground with his arrows no
more than three times;[2] if he had done so five or six times,
he would have been sure of smiting the Aramaeans—'completely'. Each of these examples well illustrates the principle of what has been called homoeopathic or imitative
magic;[3] and there is reason to believe that in Israel an acted
spell of this kind might be classed as a form of מָשָׁל (EVV.
'proverb, byword, parable').[4]

---

[1] 2 Kings xiii. 17. For תְּשׁוּעָה ('salvation'), as denoting 'victory', see Pedersen, *Israel: its Life and Culture I–II*, pp. 330 ff.

[2] Verses 18 f.

[3] J. G. Frazer, *The Golden Bough: A Study in Magic and Religion*, 3rd
edit. (1911–15), I. i, pp. 55 ff.

[4] Cf. the writer's study of this term in *Wisdom in Israel and in the Ancient
Near East* (H. H. Rowley *Festschrift*), ed. M. Noth and D. W. Thomas,
S.V.T. iii (1955), pp. 162–9, where the writer has sought to show how the
etymological implication of 'likeness' comes out in the various connotations
of the term. In short, it could be used (a) of a parallel which in fact already
existed and, therefore, might serve as an example to be shunned or followed,
as the case might be, and (b) of a parallel which was first pictured in the mind
and then given colourful expression in words alone or through some form of
symbolic action and a corresponding oral pronouncement with a view in either
case to its subsequent reproduction as an actual fact. For our present purpose
the most striking examples of the use of the term in the latter way are afforded

Further, a particularly valuable piece of evidence in this connexion is to be found in Hosea's summary of the prophetic function, when he says on behalf of Yahweh:[1]

by (i) the utterances of Balaam (Num. xxiii. 7, 18, xxiv. 3, 15, 20, 21, 23 (all JE)), and (ii) Ezek. xxiv. 3 ff., which appears to offer a relatively late example of the use of מָשָׁל with reference to an actual piece of symbolism and an accompanying exposition in words. In this case the prophet is told by Yahweh to produce a מָשָׁל (Heb.: מְשֹׁל מָשָׁל) in terms of a cauldron which, on being put into use, is found to be so rusted as to involve the turning out of its contents and its own melting down; and it is commonly recognized that we have here a simile of the siege of Jerusalem which is so dramatic in quality that the prophet's words must have been accompanied by symbolic action of the type which we know to have been a regular feature of his ministry. Cf. iv. 1 ff., v. 1 ff., vi. 11 f., xii. 1–16, 17–20, xxi. 11 f., 23 ff. (EVV. 6 f., 18 ff.), xxxvii. 15 ff.; and, for the likelihood that some form of symbolic action should be recognized in the passage under discussion, see H. Schmidt, S.A.T. ii. 2, 2nd edit. rev. (1923), J. Herrmann, K.A.T. (1924), G. A. Cooke, I.C.C. (1936), and G. Fohrer, H.A.T. (1955), *in loc.* Note, too, the use of the verb נָשָׂא, 'to raise', in the Balaam stories to describe the utterance of the מָשָׁל: cf. Isa. xiv. 4; Mic. ii. 4; Hab. ii. 6; also Job xxvii. 1, xxix. 1. It is to be compared with the use of the same verb to denote the 'raising' of the voice in wailing (e.g. Gen. xxi. 16 (E), xxvii. 38 (J); Judges xxi. 2; Ruth i. 9; 1 Sam. xxx. 4; 2 Sam. iii. 32; Job ii. 12), in rejoicing (Isa. xxiv. 14, lii. 8), in shouting a message (Judges ix. 7), &c.; and its use in the present connexion is obviously in keeping with the importance attached to the power of the spoken word. Indeed it should be borne in mind that נָשָׂא could even be used by itself to denote loud utterance (cf. Job xxi. 12; Isa. iii. 7, xlii. 2, 11); for this explains the use of the term מַשָּׂא, commonly rendered by 'burden', to denote a prophetic utterance or 'oracle'. Cf., for example, R.V. mgn. and R.S.V. ('oracle') as against A.V. and R.V. ('burden') in such passages as Isa. xiii. 1, xv. 1, xvii. 1, &c.; Nahum i. 1; Hab. i. 1; Zech. ix. 1, xii. 1; Mal. i. 1. It obviously implies something which is spoken with a 'raised' voice; and, indeed, one may speak of 'raising' (as uttering or proclaiming) a מַשָּׂא. Cf. 2 Kings ix. 25, where the Hebrew implies that the treatment to be meted out to Joram's body would be in keeping with the 'oracle' which Yahweh had 'uttered' against Ahab (cf. R.V. mgn., R.S.V.) rather than the 'burden' which Yahweh had 'laid' upon him (cf. A.V., R.V.). See also Jer. xxiii. 33 ff., where the play on these two meanings of מַשָּׂא is the key to the whole passage. For interesting but, in the present writer's opinion, unconvincing attempts to recognize in the foregoing use of the term מַשָּׂא, not a secondary derivation from √נשׂא in the sense of 'to utter', but simply the thought of a divine utterance as a 'burden' which has been imposed upon the speaker, see H. S. Gehman, 'The "Burden" of the Prophet', *J.Q.R.* xxxi (1940), pp. 107 ff., and P. A. H. de Boer, 'An Inquiry into the Meaning of the Term מַשָּׂא', *O.T.S.* v (1948), pp. 197–214, both of which should be consulted, not only for the arguments advanced, but also for their bibliographical references. See further B.D.B. and K.B., s.v.; also Haeussermann, op. cit., p. 17.

[1] xii. 11 (EVV. 10).

I was continually speaking (√דבר) to the prophets,
    Indeed I gave many a חָזוֹן;
        Yea, by means of the prophets I . . . (?)

The word left untranslated, i.e. the *Pi‘ēl* of √דמה, has
suffered considerable misunderstanding through a failure
to appreciate the fact that the ideas involved belong to the
same class as those under discussion.[1] The form in question
means literally 'to make like', and is rendered in the English Versions by 'to use similitudes' (cf. R.S.V.: 'to give
parables'). A comparative study of its use, however, reveals
the fact that it means something more than this, and that
here again one should recognize a background of what be-
gan as magical ideas. Thus, it is always found elsewhere
in the Old Testament in one of two senses: (*a*) that of 'to
compare', a rendering which is obviously unsuitable in this
case, and (*b*) that of 'to picture' something in the present
which is to happen in *the future*—and so, occasionally, of
mental processes in the sense of 'to plan'.[2] In Psalm xlviii,
however, it is used in the latter sense in a way which seems
to place its meaning in the present passage beyond dispute;

---

[1] Some editors have gone so far as to regard the reading as corrupt. Cf.,
for example, K. Marti, K.H.C. (1904), followed tentatively by W. Nowack,
H.K., 3rd edit. rev. (1922), E. Sellin, K.A.T., 2nd and 3rd edit. rev. (1929),
and J. Lippl, H.S.A.T. (1937), *in loc.* The consonantal text, however, has
the support of LXX (ὡμοιώθην: cf. S ܐܬܕܡܝܬ, V *adsimilatus sum*); so that
others, with more justification, have sought a meaning in terms of √דמה, *Qal*,
(i) 'to be silent', (ii) 'to silence (= destroy)', seeing this transitive force,
whether in the *Qal* or in the *Pi‘ēl*, as the meaning intended here by the
speaker. Cf., for example, J. Wellhausen, *Die kleinen Propheten*, 3rd edit.
(1898), A. van Hoonacker, E.B. (1908), T. H. Robinson, H.A.T., 2nd edit.
rev. (1954), A. Weiser, A.T.D., 2nd edit. rev. (1956), and F. Nötscher,
Echt.B., 2nd edit. rev. (1958), *in loc.* This, however, fails to do justice to the
parallelism; and the traditional association of the form under discussion with
√דמה *Qal*, 'to be like' (cf. A.V., R.V., and R.S.V., as cited later in the text), is
rightly retained by G. A. Smith, *The Book of the Twelve Prophets*, 2nd edit.
rev. (1928), p. 330, and W. R. Harper, I.C.C. (1905), *in loc.*, both of whom
treat the Hebrew as meaning 'to give parables' (i.e. *qua* 'similitudes': cf.
Harper); similarly H. Guthe, *H.S.A.T.* (1923), and D. Deden, B.O.T.
(1953), *in loc.*

[2] (*a*) Song of Sol. i. 9; Isa. xl. 18, 25, xlvi. 5; Lam. ii. 13: (*b*) Num. xxxiii.
56 (P); Judges xx. 5; 2 Sam. xxi. 5; Esther iv. 13; Pss. xlviii. 10 (EVV. 9),
l. 21; Isa. x. 7, xiv. 24.

for the fact is that, if justice is to be done to the language of the psalm as a whole, it becomes intelligible only when it is seen in the context of a ritual drama in which Yahweh is represented as overthrowing the earthly kings who threaten the life of His people.[1] The dramatic element is already indicated in the lines:[2]

> As we have heard, so have we seen
> In the city of Yahweh of Hosts,
> In the city of our God (*or* in our divine city),
> Which God maintaineth for ever.

It is, therefore, highly significant to find that the verbal form under discussion is used in the following line to explain what has been taking place:

> O God, we have pictured Thy devotion[3]
> In the midst of Thy Temple.

The context shows, however, that this depicting of the future is something more than a mere mental picture. It belongs rather to that type of acted 'picture' which is connected with the above-mentioned practice of homoeopathic magic or the influence of 'like' upon 'like',[4] although in this particular case one must recognize the transition to a mimetic ritual which, with its attendant psalmody, is to prove effective, not in any magical way, but through its influence upon the minds and hearts of the worshippers.[5]

---

[1] Cf. S. Mowinckel, *Psalmenstudien II. Das Thronbesteigungsfest Jahwäs und der Ursprung der Eschatologie*, S.N.V.A.O. II, 1921, No. 6 (1922), pp. 61 ff., 126 ff., and the present writer's essay, 'The Rôle of the King in the Jerusalem Cultus', in *The Labyrinth*, ed. S. H. Hooke (1935), pp. 92 ff.: but see now *Sacral Kingship in Ancient Israel*, pp. 77 ff., where the argument of the foregoing essay has been developed and, in part, modified by an emphasis upon the eschatological rather than the cyclic aspect of the ritual under review. Further, the writer is glad to have had the opportunity of expanding his treatment of √דמה within such a context as the above, for it should serve to meet the criticism of J. Morgenstern in his full and informative exposition of Psalm xlviii, *H.U.C.A.* xvi (1941), pp. 1–95, i.e. p. 92. Cf., too, the writer's comments on this point in *E.T.* lxviii (1956–7), p. 179.

[2] Verse 9 (EVV. 8).

[3] See above, p. 5, n. 6.

[4] Cf. T. Mainage, *Religions de la préhistoire* (1921), p. 339.

[5] Cf. *Sacral Kingship in Ancient Israel*, pp. 129 f.

Accordingly it is this range of ideas which is implied by the use of the same verbal form in the above passage from Hosea,[1] which emphasizes the fact (and this is the actual testimony of Hosea) that the prophets are Yahweh's instruments in fashioning the future; their actions and words have creative (or destructive)[2] power. Moreover, this interpretation finds confirmation in the fact that the term under discussion is used more or less as a parallel to the terminology of the חָזוֹן / דָּבָר (or 'word' / 'observation'); and it has already been shown that this conception has roots in the soil of magical ideas. Finally, the latitude which must be allowed in one's interpretation of the term חָזוֹן, as being practically synonymous with דָּבָר and, therefore, to be rendered by 'observation' rather than 'vision', is also made clear by Jeremiah when he says:[3]

Thus saith Yahweh of Hosts!
  Do not listen to the 'words' (דְּבָרִים) of the prophets
    Who prophesy to (*or* for) you.

[1] Cf. Guillaume, op. cit., p. 138, n. 1, who follows the traditional rendering (i.e. 'to use similitudes') but recognizes that Hosea's words 'could apply to all similitudes, e.g. the acted sign'.

[2] Cf., perhaps, Hos. vi. 5, where Yahweh apparently recalls the way in which He has sought to shape His people by repeated acts of judgement exercised through His prophets:

　　　Therefore I have hewn by means of the prophets,
　　　　I have slain them by the utterances of My Mouth,
　　　　⌈My judgement⌉ issuing forth ⌈like⌉ the light.

Cf. R.V. mgn., and R.S.V. (following LXX, S, and T, with a different division of the consonants from that of M.T. in the last stichos); and see further, for example, Harper, op. cit., *in loc.* It must be admitted, however, that the syntax of the first two stichoi, which are our immediate concern, is somewhat uncertain; and it is possible to translate the passage as follows:

　　　Therefore I have hewn among the prophets,
　　　　I have slain them by the utterances of My Mouth,
　　　　　&c.

Cf., for example, Sellin, op cit., *in loc.* (with corresponding attention to the renderings of LXX and S). In view of the parallelism the ambiguity would be lessened in favour of the first interpretation, if one could regard the suffixed 'them' in the second stichos as due to the misunderstanding of an enclitic -*m*. Cf. Ps. lxxxv. 4 (EVV. 3), as cited by H. D. Hummel, 'Enclitic *mem* in Early Northwest Semitic, especially Hebrew', *J.B.L.* lxxvi (1957), p. 103; but see G. R. Driver, *Canaanite Myths and Legends*, O.T.S. 3 (1956), p. 130, n. 2.　　　　　　　　　　　　　　　[3] xxiii. 16.

These men are only fooling you;
  It is an 'observation' (חָזוֹן) from their own heart that they speak,
  Not one out of the Mouth of Yahweh.

This reference to a חָזוֹן as coming from the Mouth of Yahweh offers an exact parallel to that of the sixth-century
writer, mentioned above,[1] who similarly refers to the דָּבָר
as going forth from the Mouth of Yahweh to perform that
which He pleases.[2]

  Again, the passage quoted above is but one of a whole
series of utterances directed against the contemporary prophets; and it is to be observed that Jeremiah's condemnation

---

[1] pp. 38 f.
[2] Cf. Prov. xxix. 18, where the importance of the חָזוֹן as a form of תּוֹרָה is
clearly expressed, i.e.:
  Where there is no חָזוֹן a people will run wild;
  But happy is the one that heedeth תּוֹרָה.
Note (a) the parallelism, and (b) the fact that the term תּוֹרָה was not restricted
to priestly 'direction'. See above, p. 7, n. 5, and cf. the rendering of R.S.V.:
  Where there is no prophecy the people cast off restraint,
  but blessed is he who keeps the law.
This is an improvement on the familiar rendering of the EVV. so far as the
first stichos is concerned, although it has probably been the cause of some
surprise among those who have been wont to take the familiar words of the
A.V. and R.V. (i.e. 'Where there is no vision . . .') in an unduly subjective
way. Nevertheless it seems to the writer that even the R.S.V. may be misleading in so far as the continued rendering of תּוֹרָה in the second stichos
by 'the law' (italics mine, A.R.J.) may appear to justify the view that in this
proverb we have a reference to (i) the canonical 'Prophets', and (ii) the
Pentateuch as being 'The Law' *par excellence*. Admittedly this is the view
which has been commonly held by commentators, who have thought accordingly, but in the writer's opinion quite unwarrantably, of the first steps in the
formation of the Old Testament canon and, therefore, of a very late date
for this particular proverb. Cf., for example, G. Wildeboer, K.H.C. (1897),
C. Steuernagel, *H.S.A.T.* (1923), W. O. E. Oesterley, W.C. (1929), and C. T.
Fritsch, I.B. (1955), *in loc.* Nevertheless the use of the word חָזוֹן, as discussed
above in the text, surely points to the fact that the author of this proverb had
in mind the thought of divine guidance given through the spoken word
rather than written records of such guidance which had been preserved over
the years because of their authority in terms of divine revelation. Cf. what
the writer regards as the more satisfactory treatment of this passage by B.
Gemser, H.A.T. (1937), H. Duesberg and P. Auvray, S.B.J., 2nd edit. rev.
(1957), and V. Hamp, Echt.B., 2nd edit. rev. (1959), *in loc.* (Note incidentally
that, as it seems to the writer, the singular forms of the second stichos should
be construed in a collective sense as being parallel to the term עַם, 'people',
in the first stichos.)

centres in the assertion that normally their oracles are either the product of their own imagination[1] or the result of mere dreams.[2] Jeremiah himself, apparently, did not regard the latter as a valid medium of revelation;[3] but this was far from being the common point of view.[4] Thus dreams are a frequent and recognized medium of revelation in the work of E;[5] and in Numbers xii. 6 (JE) they are classed as such along with visions, when Yahweh says:

> Hear now My 'Word'![6]
> If your prophet be (from) Yahweh,[7]
> It is in a vision (מַרְאָה) that I make Myself known to him,
> It is in a dream that I speak with him.

[1] Cf. verses 16 (as above) and 26.

[2] Verses 25 ff.

[3] Cf., for example, H. W. Hertzberg, *Prophet und Gott: Eine Studie zur Religiosität des vorexilischen Prophetentums*, B.F.C.T. 28. 3 (1923), pp. 219 ff.; Quell, op. cit., pp. 162 ff.; E. L. Ehrlich, *Der Traum im Alten Testament*, B.Z.A.W. 73 (1953), pp. 155 ff.: as against Hänel, op. cit., pp. 132 ff.

[4] Cf. Hänel, op. cit., pp. 128 ff.; Dhorme, *R.H.R.* cviii (1933), pp. 124 ff., *L'Évolution religieuse d'Israël. I: La Religion des Hébreux nomades*, pp. 231 ff.; Guillaume, op. cit., pp. 213 ff.; Ehrlich, op. cit., *passim*.

[5] See the cautious treatment of this point by Ehrlich, op. cit., *passim*, notably pp. 125–36.

[6] A.V., R.V., and R.S.V., following the Massoretic vocalization, render by a plural; but the consonantal text may be read equally well as a singular.

[7] i.e. if he be a true prophet. Editors commonly (*a*) reject יהוה as an intrusion into the text, either as a gloss or by misplacement, and (*b*) follow the lead of V by reading נָבִיא בָּכֶם for נְבִיאֲכֶם, thus securing the rendering, 'If there be a prophet among you.' Cf., for example, H. Holzinger, K.H.C. (1903), p. 46, and *H.S.A.T.* (1922), *in loc.*, who in the former case offers a summary of views to date; G. B. Gray, I.C.C. (1903), and A. H. McNeile, C.B. (1911), *in loc.*, who rightly point out that there is no justification for construing 'Yahweh' as the appositional subject of 'I make Myself known' (i.e. 'I, Yahweh, make Myself known'), as is done by EVV. (cf., too, R.S.V.); also P. Heinisch, H.S.A.T. (1936), H. Cazelles, S.B.J., 2nd edit. rev. (1958), and, in part, H. Schneider, Echt.B., 2nd edit. rev. (1955). The M.T. appears to have the support of LXX, i.e. ἐὰν γένηται προφήτης ὑμῶν Κυρίῳ, where the translator seems to have done his best with a text which must have been as perplexing to him as it is for the modern reader; and it is generally agreed, of course, that the Hebrew can only mean, 'If your prophet be Yahweh'. This is regularly dismissed as nonsense; but is it quite so nonsensical as it appears? Cf. *The One and the Many in the Israelite Conception of God*, pp. 36 ff., 2nd edit., pp. 32 ff., where it is shown (i) that the true prophet, in delivering his message, could be regarded, like the 'Angel' of Yahweh, as virtually Yahweh 'in Person', and (ii) that the type of oscillation which appears in these lines,

Further, the prophets whom Jeremiah denounces (and, incidentally, they seem fairly numerous) were apparently quite frank in saying[1]

> I have dreamed, I have dreamed,

when they gave what was supposed to be a message from Yahweh; and the people in general must have believed in the validity of the claim or they would not have been led astray in the manner of which Jeremiah complains.[2]

Moreover (and this is a point of first importance), it is not to be supposed that Jeremiah makes a sweeping condemnation of the contemporary prophets on the ground that they function wholly without authority. As a matter of fact he himself reveals that their authority may be quite as valid as his own. He makes this clear when he says, speaking in the Name of Yahweh:[3]

> The prophet that hath a dream,
> Let him relate a dream;
> But one that hath My 'Word',
> Let him speak My 'Word' faithfully.

Jeremiah makes this still clearer, however, and incidentally throws an even greater light upon the activity of the prophets, when he says:[4]

> Therefore, behold, I am against the prophets
> —Oracle of Yahweh!—
> Who steal My 'Words' from one another!

according as the speaker is transmitting his message in the 'Person' of Yahweh and thus uses the 1st person *or* is doing so in a more detached way by referring to Him in the 3rd person, is a characteristic feature of prophetic utterances; indeed it recurs in the following verses, as given below, p. 48. Hence, despite the seeming absurdity, it is by no means certain that the Hebrew would have been inconceivable on the lips of an early Israelite or unintelligible in his ears; and, indeed, it may be argued that the construction has a close parallel in Ps. xlv. 7 (EVV. 6), as discussed in *Sacral Kingship in Ancient Israel*, p. 27, n. 1. Accordingly the writer hesitates to regard the text as corrupt, and certainly rejects as far too drastic the emendation referred to above. Two simpler possibilities lie before one, i.e. either (*a*) to read נְבִיאֲךָ מֵיהוה (cf. G.K. § 128*d*), assuming that the consonantal text has been wrongly divided, and explaining the resultant change from the plural to the singular of address in terms of the corresponding oscillation which is discussed op. cit., *passim*; or (*b*) to read מֵיהוה for יהוה on the ground of haplography.

[1] Verse 25. [2] Verse 32. [3] Verse 28. [4] Verse 30.

In making such a statement Jeremiah recognizes that these oracles which the prophets steal from one another are the genuine 'Words' of Yahweh; and he, therefore, makes it plain that it is not their office but the abuse of that office which he condemns.[1] This quotation, however, is even more illuminating, for it offers further evidence of the fact, already emphasized by Micah a century earlier, that there is a regular traffic in oracles akin to that which is found elsewhere in the ancient world.[2] The Delphic Oracle is a famous instance which comes easily to mind; and in this connexion the contrast drawn in Numbers xii. 6 ff. (JE) between Moses and the typical prophet is worth noting. Thus, as already observed,[3] it is said that Yahweh reveals Himself to the latter in visions and dreams; but

> My servant Moses is not like that;
>   *He* can be trusted anywhere within My House!
> It is mouth to mouth that I speak with him,
>   In plain view and not in riddles;
>   Yea, he can see the very Figure of Yahweh!

It seems an obvious inference from this picturesque description of the prophets as relative outsiders by comparison with Moses that their oracles, like those of the Pythia at Delphi,[4] were often conveniently enigmatic. Moreover, it is highly significant that the prophets could be accused of stealing them from one another. Like those of the canonical prophets, they were obviously preserved in some way;[5] and,

---

[1] See again what is said above, p. 31, n. 1, with regard to easy generalizations about 'true' and 'false' prophets.

[2] This being the case, there is almost a suggestion of sarcasm in the statement that, when Samuel was a youth, the דְּבַר of Yahweh was rare; there was no outbreak of חָזוֹן (1 Sam. iii. 1). See above, p. 13; but note G. R. Driver's view that the Hebrew of the second half of this statement can mean only that 'there was no vision ordained (*sc.* by God)': cf. *J.T.S.* xxiii (1921–2), pp. 72 f., xxxii (1930–1), p. 365.

[3] See above, p. 46.

[4] For the classical references, see Dempsey, *The Delphic Oracle*, p. 66, n. 4; Parke and Wormell, *The Delphic Oracle*, i, p. 40. Cf., too, Apuleius, *Metamorphoses*, ix. 8, with reference to the oracular responses given by the wandering 'priests' of the Dea Syria (referred to above, p. 20).

[5] See below, p. 62.

this being the case, it would be an easy matter for them to be used again—not always, apparently, by those who originally uttered them. This, taken in conjunction with the fact that the prophets could also be accused of claiming divine authority for what were really their own thoughts, is important; for it suggests that one must beware of laying too great an emphasis upon the possibility of so-called 'ecstatic' or abnormal experiences on their part.

Further, this widespread traffic in oracles, which had continued unabated in Jerusalem for more than a century, was due to the fact that the prophets were regularly consulted on matters relating to one's personal welfare; for these consultative specialists are condemned, alike by Micah in the eighth century B.C. and by Jeremiah and Ezekiel a hundred or more years later, for leading the people astray by giving them quite unwarranted promises of 'Peace (שָׁלוֹם)!'[1] Indeed, in view of the importance attached (at least in some measure) to the effectiveness of the prophetic utterance, it is not too much to say that the prophets were consulted for the sake of securing such welfare;[2] and, what is more, the welfare in question might be that of an individual

[1] 'Peace', which is the traditional rendering of שָׁלוֹם, really has a somewhat misleading suggestion of passivity in this connexion. The Hebrew term has a more active meaning, and is thus more forceful; it denotes an ordered or harmonious functioning of the whole personality, individual or collective (cf. p. 50, n. 1), and may be rendered more appropriately by 'welfare'. Cf. Pedersen, op. cit., pp. 263 ff.

[2] This point needs emphasis, as it throws light upon the antithesis which is commonly made as between the so-called 'false' prophets, acting in concert as 'prophets of weal' (*Heilspropheten*), and those who, like Micaiah and certain of the canonical prophets, are found to act independently and characteristically as 'prophets of woe' (*Unheilspropheten*). Cf. 1 Kings xxii (2 Chron. xviii); and see further, for example, H. Gressmann, *Der Messias* (1929), pp. 77 ff.; H. Gunkel, *R.G.G.*² iv (1930), art. 'Propheten' II.B., 2. a. It should be realized that it was the function of the cultic prophets to *create* the שָׁלוֹם or 'peace' which they were apparently promising so glibly; and that is why so much attention has been given in the preceding pages to the power attributed to their actions and utterances. At the same time one must beware of overemphasizing this magical (or, rather, quasi-magical) aspect; it remains to be seen whether or not such apparent promises of 'Peace!' were ever given under the recognition that they were morally conditioned. See p. 22, n. 1, *ad fin.*

or that of a social unit or 'corporate personality'[1] such as the city of Jerusalem or the kingdom of Judah.[2]

Thus, just as Micah denounces his contemporaries amongst the prophets for giving such oracles of 'Peace!' to anyone prepared to pay enough for them, so Jeremiah, in pronouncing Yahweh's condemnation of those of his own time for speaking an 'observation' out of their own heart instead of an authoritative one from His Mouth, concludes with the statement:[3]

They continually say to those who spurn Me,
  'Yahweh hath said, Ye shall have peace![4]'
And, as for every one that walketh in the stubbornness of his heart,
  They say, 'No evil shall come upon you!'

Similarly the prophetic responsibility for the welfare of the social unit (or corporate, as distinct from individual, personality) finds ample illustration, as when Jeremiah thus voices Yahweh's protest:[5]

As for both prophet and priest,
  Every one doth what is false;
They would heal the hurt of My people lightly,
  Saying 'Peace!' 'Peace!'—when there is no peace.[6]

Again, in another passage (which incidentally offers an excellent illustration of a canonical prophet approaching Yahweh for guidance)[7] Jeremiah adds:[8]

Then I said,
  O Yahweh, my Lord, look how the prophets say unto them:
  'Ye shall not see the sword, nor shall ye have famine;
  But I will give you true peace in this place.'
Then Yahweh said to me,

---

[1] Cf. H. W. Robinson, 'Hebrew Psychology', in *The People and the Book*, ed. A. S. Peake (1925), pp. 353–82, particularly 375 ff.; and 'The Hebrew Conception of Corporate Personality', in *Werden und Wesen des Alten Testaments*, ed. J. Hempel, B.Z.A.W. 66 (1936), pp. 49–62. See also *The One and the Many in the Israelite Conception of God*, pp. 11 ff., 2nd edit., pp. 7 ff.

[2] See again p. 22, n. 1, *ad fin.*   [3] xxiii. 17: see above, pp. 44 f.
[4] i.e. 'You will be all right!'   [5] vi. 13 f.: cf. viii. 10 f.
[6] i.e. ' "It's all right!" "It's all right!"—when it is not all right.'
[7] See below, pp. 58 f.   [8] xiv. 13 f.

The prophets prophesy falsely in My Name;
I have not sent them, nor have I commanded them, nor have I
  spoken unto them.
It is a false 'observation' and worthless 'divination'
And their own deceitful thoughts that they prophesy unto you.

Such a record, indeed, is of the first importance; for it reveals Jeremiah as standing in opposition to a company of
prophets (how numerous it is impossible to say) who are
characterized by the fact, not simply that they give oracles
of 'Peace!', but that they do so with a claim to authority
similar to his own—that of speaking in the Name of Yahweh. In the same way Ezekiel, who in a collection of utterances against contemporary prophets likewise condemns
them for their futile 'observations' and lying 'divination',
voices an indignant complaint that the people as a whole
(the corporate personality represented by the city of Jerusalem) have been led astray through these unwarranted
promises of 'Peace!' Indeed, having likened the people in
general to folk who build a wall and the prophets in particular to those who come along and coat it over with whitewash,
he proceeds to threaten destruction of their joint but futile
labour, and concludes (speaking in the Name of Yahweh):[1]

Thus I will expend My wrath against the wall and against those
who coated it over with whitewash; so that I may say to you, 'The
wall is no more, nor those who coated it over with whitewash—
namely, the prophets of Israel who prophesied unto Jerusalem and
kept making for her an "observation" of "Peace!", when there was
no peace.'
Oracle of Yahweh, my Lord!

This means that in the last resort it is the prophets rather
than the people in general who are to be blamed for disaster,[2] inasmuch as the latter are not in a position to distinguish
the true from the false oracle; for all are given with an
equal claim to authority in the Name of Yahweh. Jeremiah
suggests as much;[3] but Ezekiel makes it doubly clear. Thus,

---

[1] xiii. 15 f.   [2] Cf. Lam. ii. 14: and see below, pp. 66 ff.
[3] As above, p. 50, n. 8.

in making a general denunciation of the national leaders, he again uses the above simile with reference to the prophets, and says:[1]

Her prophets have coated over with whitewash for them,
 Making futile 'observations' and offering them lying 'divination',
Saying 'Thus saith Yahweh, my Lord!',
 Although Yahweh hath not spoken.

In much the same way he complains that:[2]

 Their 'observations' were nothing but lying 'divination',[3]
  Who said 'Oracle of Yahweh!',
 Although Yahweh had not sent them,
  And so expected to make a דָּבָר effective!

When *all* prophets sought to substantiate their oracles by means of the formulae 'Thus saith Yahweh!' (כֹּה אָמַר יהוה) or 'Oracle of Yahweh!' (נְאֻם יהוה),[4] it was obviously difficult to distinguish the true from the false. Originally, of course, a 'sign' (אוֹת) or 'portent' (מוֹפֵת), whether of an ordinary or of a miraculous kind,[5] was offered as a guarantee of reliability.[6] The use of this device is recorded, not only on one occasion of Samuel the 'seer'[7] and on more than one occasion

---

[1] xxii. 28: cf. Jer. xxiii. 31, 33 ff.

[2] xiii. 6: see above, p. 36, n. 5. Note the sarcastic reference to the attempted substantiation of the דָּבָר (as above, p. 38, n. 5).

[3] *lit.* 'They "observed" nothing but lying "divination".' For the syntax of this clause as a whole, cf. Lam. ii. 14, as quoted below, pp. 67 f.

[4] For a discussion of these formulae, see Haeussermann, op. cit., pp. 12 ff.

[5] See (*a*) for the ordinary type with אוֹת, 1 Sam. ii. 34, x. 1 (cf. LXX, V)–13; 2 Kings xix. 29 (= Isa. xxxvii. 30); Isa. vii. 10 ff.; Jer. xliv. 29 f.; cf. Exod. iii. 12 (E): (*b*) for the miraculous type with אוֹת, 2 Kings xx. 8 ff. (cf. Isa. xxxviii. 7 f., 22); also Exod. iv. 1 ff. (JE); Judges vi. 17 ff.: for the miraculous type with מוֹפֵת Exod. iv. 21 (JE), vii. 9 (P); 1 Kings xiii. 3, 5; 2 Chron. xxxii. 24, 31 (cf. 2 Kings xx. 8 ff., as above). Cf., too, the general references to both terms in Deut. xiii. 2 f. (EVV. 1 f.), as cited below, p. 53, n. 5.

[6] Cf. Keller, *Das Wort OTH als 'Offenbarungszeichen Gottes'*, pp. 51 ff., 60 f., although the present writer is unable to accept the author's main thesis, i.e. that the word אוֹת was originally a sacral term which came into secular use only at a comparatively late date. This theory is difficult to substantiate when the available evidence is not only comparatively meagre but also, itself, almost wholly religious in character.

[7] 1 Sam. x. 7, 9 (אוֹת): cf. x. 1 (LXX, V).

of an unnamed 'man of God',[1] but also of certain of the
canonical prophets;[2] and, indeed, there is a significant parallel in the traditions of the Exodus as conveyed by the JE
strand of the Pentateuch, which tells of more than one
'sign' (אוֹת) which was to be wrought by Moses in confirmation of his claim to be Yahweh's messenger to the en-
slaved Hebrews[3]—a claim which was made by one who in
Israelite sacred story was the outstanding 'man of God' or
'prophet'.[4] On the other hand, such use of an אוֹת or a מוֹפֵת
is severely criticized in the work of the D school, where it
is explicitly stated that this device may be misleading, and
that it is in the fulfilment or non-fulfilment of an oracle
that one is to distinguish the true from the false prophet;[5]

---

[1] 1 Sam. ii. 34 (אוֹת); 1 Kings xiii. 3, 5 (מוֹפֵת): cf. Deut. xiii. 2 f. (EVV. 1 f.);
Judges vi. 17. The expression 'man of God' is a synonym for 'seer' or
'prophet': cf. 1 Sam. ix. 1–x. 16, esp. ix. 6–10; 1 Kings xiii. 11 ff., esp. 18;
2 Kings v, esp. 8; and so often.

[2] Notably Isaiah, i.e. 2 Kings xix. 29, xx. 8 f.; Isa. vii. 11, 14, xxxviii. 7,
22, 30 (all with אוֹת): cf. 2 Chron. xxxii. 24, 31 (both with מוֹפֵת). See also Jer.
xliv. 29 (with אוֹת). Such instances are to be distinguished, of course, from
those in which the אוֹת or מוֹפֵת has a symbolic character and is probably to be
regarded as a form of מָשָׁל (cf. p. 40, n. 4), although in these cases, no doubt,
the action in question was to be effective only in virtue of the lesson which it
was designed to convey. Cf. Isa. viii. 18, xx. 3 (both terms in each case);
Ezek. iv. 3 (אוֹת), xii. 6, 11, xxiv. 24, 27 (all מוֹפֵת): also Zech. iii. 8 (מוֹפֵת). See
further Keller, op. cit., pp. 49 ff., 60 f., 94 ff.; and note that the writer hopes
to deal with the use of the term אוֹת in Pss. lxxiv. 9 (cf. verse 4?) and lxxxvi. 17,
as discussed by Keller, op. cit., pp. 43 ff., in the immediate sequel to this work.

[3] Exod. iv. 8 f., 17, 28, 30 (JE). The reader should note in passing how the
Hebrew of verse 8 draws attention to the thought of these signs as bearers of
a message or, perhaps one may say, as designed to have a telling effect. This
may be seen in the literal translations of both A.V. and R.V. (i.e. 'the voice
of the first sign' and 'the voice of the latter sign'), but it appears to have been
ignored by the translators of R.S.V. in the interests of a smoother rendering.
Cf., too, Ps. cv. 27, e.g. A.V. mgn. and R.V. mgn. ('the words of his signs')
as opposed to the simpler renderings of A.V., R.V., and R.S.V. ('his signs').

[4] Cf. Num. xii. 6 ff. (JE), as discussed above, p. 48: also (a) Deut. xxxiii. 1;
Joshua xiv. 6; (b) Deut. xxxiv. 10.

[5] Cf. Deut. xiii. 2–6 (EVV. 1–5), xviii. 21 f.; also, similarly, Jer. xxviii. 9:
and see further J. Skinner, *Prophecy and Religion* (1922), pp. 186 ff. It should
be borne in mind in this connexion that the plagues of Egypt, which figure
as 'signs' and 'portents' in D quite as strongly as they do elsewhere in the
O.T., were regarded as such, not because they served as Moses' credentials,
but because they enjoyed a special significance as belonging to that type of
event which a prophet might cite as evidence of Yahweh's power over nature

but this evidently represents a reaction against current practice which by the very fact of its occurrence illustrates afresh the value that was commonly attached to a 'sign' or 'portent' as testimony to the truth of a prophetic utterance. All in all, therefore, the importance of these statements can scarcely be exaggerated; they serve to emphasize the fact that the canonical prophets, if their work is to be understood aright, must be seen against a wide background of prophetic activity—particularly in Jerusalem. On the testimony of the canonical prophets themselves it is evident that there was a large number of prophets forming a class of consultative specialists; and moreover, as such, they made an equal claim to act and speak authoritatively, and therefore effectively, in the Name of Yahweh.

This use of the 'Name', so important an 'Extension' of the divine Personality,[1] is another notable aspect of the prophetic function; and here again, as in the foregoing sarcastic statement by Ezekiel for instance,[2] it is possible to discern the lingering on of some such magical or quasi-magical idea as that which is occasionally, if only faintly, suggested by the expression commonly rendered in the A.V., R.V., and R.S.V. as 'calling upon the name of the Lord'.[3] As is well known, this is used, not only to denote

and in the realm of history, using it for its telling effect as yet another method of driving home the particular lesson which he had to convey. Cf. (although sometimes a very general reference to the 'signs' and 'portents' performed in Egypt may be held to include the few instances of the type referred to above, p. 52, n. 5) Exod. vii. 3 (P), viii. 19 (EVV. 23) (J), x. 1 f. (J), xi. 9 f. (P); Deut. iv. 34, vi. 22, vii. 19, xi. 3, xxvi. 8, xxix. 2 (EVV. 3), xxxiv. 11; Joshua xxiv. 17 (JE); Neh. ix. 10; Pss. lxxviii. 43, cv. 27 (as cited above, p. 53, n. 3, *ad fin.*), cxxxv. 9; Jer. xxxii. 20 f.: also, with other or more general reference, Num. xiv. 11, 22 (JE); Deut. xxviii. 46; Pss. lxv. 9 (EVV. 8), cv. 5 (= 1 Chron. xvi. 12); Isa. lxvi. 19; Ezek. xiv. 8 (cf. Ps. lxxi. 7); Joel iii. 3 (EVV. ii. 30). We may also regard as a simple form of this type of 'sign' the lay method of obtaining immediate guidance from Yahweh by using what an outsider would regard as a purely fortuitous action amid the events forming the situation in question. Cf. Gen. xxiv. 12–14 (J), and, with explicit reference to such an action as a 'sign' (אוֹת), 1 Sam. xiv. 8 ff.

[1] See above, p. 38, n. 6.
[2] See above, p. 52, n. 2.
[3] Cf. *The One and the Many in the Israelite Conception of God*, pp. 21 ff., 2nd edit., pp. 17 ff.

the invoking of Yahweh in particular cultic acts, whether in supplication or in praise,[1] but also as the normal idiom for engaging in formal worship;[2] but it should be borne in mind that this expression really means 'to call *with* the name "Yahweh" '. In other words, the basic idea is that of 'calling out the name "Yahweh" ', as is clear from its use by Yahweh Himself in connexion with the promised theophany to Moses in Exodus xxxiii. 19 f. (J):[3]

'I will see that I pass in front of thee in all My splendour;[4] I will also call out the name "Yahweh" in front of thee. Thus I shall deal graciously with one with whom I would deal graciously, and I shall show sympathy with one for whom I would show sympathy. But', He said, 'thou canst not see My Face, for mankind may not see Me and live.'

---

[1] See Gen. xii. 8, xiii. 4, xxi. 33, xxvi. 25 (all J); 1 Kings xviii. 24 (cf. verses 25 f., and see below in the text); 2 Kings v. 11 (as quoted below in the text); Ps. cxvi. 4, 13, 17; Joel iii. 5 (EVV. ii. 32): also Ps. cv. 1 (= 1 Chron. xvi. 8); Isa. xii. 4; Zech. xiii. 9.

[2] See Gen. iv. 26 (J); Zeph. iii. 9: also Pss. lxxix. 6 (cf. Jer. x. 25), lxxx. 19 (EVV. 18); Isa. xli. 25, lxiv. 6 (EVV. 7), lxv. 1 (cf. LXX, S, V, T).

[3] It is a matter of dispute as to whether or not Exod. xxxiv. 5 (J) offers a parallel to this utterance by Yahweh of the divine Name for the purpose of self-revelation. Cf. A.V., R.V., and R.S.V.: as against R.V. mgn., which implies that Moses, not Yahweh, is the subject of the verb in question. The present writer inclines to the former view, although the latter is the one which is favoured by commentators (with or without recourse to literary analysis): e.g. H. Holzinger, K.H.C. (1900), and *H.S.A.T.* (1922); B. Baentsch, H.K. (1903); S. R. Driver, C.B. (1911); A. H. McNeile, W.C., 2nd edit. rev. (1917); H. Gressmann, S.A.T., 2nd edit. rev. (1922); F. M. Th. Böhl, T.U. (1928); P. Heinisch, H.S.A.T. (1934); G. Beer, H.A.T. (1939); H. Schneider, Echt.B., 2nd edit. rev. (1955); B. Couroyer, S.B.J., 2nd edit. rev. (1959); also C. A. Simpson, *The Early Traditions of Israel* (1948), pp. 210 f.

[4] *lit.* 'I will make all My goodliness pass before thee' (cf. EVV.); but the suffixed form of טוֹב (EVV. 'goodness') here has something of the reflexive force which is to be seen in the suffixed form of פָּנִים (*lit.* 'face': EVV. 'presence') in verses 14 f. (J) and the suffixed form of כָּבוֹד (EVV. 'glory') in verse 18 (J), i.e. (i) 'I Myself will go along', and 'If Thou Thyself go not along', (ii) 'Prithee, show me Thy glorious Self'. Indeed the pronominal force of the Hebrew in the latter case has a close parallel in our own use of the expressions 'Your Honour' and 'Your Majesty'; and, while something of the force of the original would undoubtedly be lost if the Hebrew were translated simply 'Please, let me see Your Majesty', it really means little more than this. Cf. *The Vitality of the Individual in the Thought of Ancient Israel*, p. 46, n. 3, and p. 76, n. 10.

Perhaps the most graphic example of the importance which was attached to the analogous calling out of the divine 'Name' by the suppliant is to be found in the story of Elijah's contest with the prophets who played so active a part in the cultus of the Tyrian Baal; for the victory was to lie with the god whose 'name' could be invoked so effectively as to bring about the kindling of the altar fire. Thus Elijah (likewise a prophet) challenged his opponents with the words:[1]

> You shall invoke the 'name' of your god, and I will invoke Yahweh's 'Name'; and the god that answereth with fire shall be God.

In short, whatever else one might do or say in pursuit of the desired end, it was the invocation of the divine 'name' which was of basic importance in each case, if there was to be any hope of making an effective approach to the object of one's worship. In exactly the same way Naaman expected to find Yahweh's 'Name' effective on the lips of Elisha (yet another prophet), when he sought the latter's aid in being cleansed of his leprosy. Thus he thought:[2]

> He will, of course, come out to me, stand and invoke the 'Name' of Yahweh his God, wave his hand towards the place, and so remove the leprosy.

In the light of these examples it is possible to understand something of the potency attributed to the divine 'Name' by those later prophets who thought, as Ezekiel said, that they need only add 'Oracle of Yahweh!' in order to make their words effective. Indeed, one may even see something of a quondam transition from the simple spell to prayer on the one hand and oracle on the other; for as a consultative specialist the prophet, like the priest,[3] had a dual role. It was his responsibility (*a*) to call with (*or* upon) the 'Name' of Yahweh,[4] and (*b*) to speak in His 'Name'.[5]

---

[1] 1 Kings xviii. 24.   [2] 2 Kings v. 11.

[3] See above, pp. 4 ff.

[4] It may be worthy of note that the כֹּהֵן or 'priest' is nowhere explicitly referred to in the Old Testament as 'calling upon the "Name" of Yahweh'.

[5] See Deut. xviii. 19, 20, 22; 1 Kings xxii. 16 (= 2 Chron. xviii. 15); 1 Chron. xxi. 19; 2 Chron. xxxiii. 18; Jer. xx. 9, xxvi. 16, xliv. 16; Zech.

The latter or oracular aspect of the prophetic function is, of course, the one which is generally recognized. As a result of his powers in this respect the prophet, like the priest,[1] was regarded as a special source of knowledge. Nevertheless there is a marked difference between his knowledge and that of the latter. To be sure, it was often secured as a result of divination; and therefore, in this respect at least, both types of knowledge were more or less on the same plane. More often, however, it was emphasized as being due to direct personal contact with Yahweh; and on such an occasion it stands in definite contrast with the traditional lore of the priest. Amos may have insisted that he was no professional prophet;[2] but, nevertheless, he admitted that the function of the latter was quite valid, and in a noteworthy passage he has laid stress upon the close relation which existed between the prophets and Yahweh:[3]

Yahweh, my Lord, doth nothing (i.e. performeth no דָּבָר)[4]
> Without revealing His intimate counsel to His servants the
> prophets.

Jeremiah draws a somewhat similar picture when, speaking in the Name of Yahweh, he thus denounces the prophets of his own day:[5]

> I did not send the prophets,
>> Although they ran.
> I did not speak to them,
>> Although they prophesied.
> If they had really stood in My intimate Council,

xiii. 3 (as below, p. 66, n. 1): also Dan. ix. 6. Cf., too, Exod. v. 23 (J), of Moses: also Jer. xi. 21, xxvi. 9, 20 (cf. xiv. 14, 15, xxiii. 25, xxvii. 15, xxix. 9, 21), of prophesying in the 'Name' of Yahweh. In view of what is said in the following paragraph about the type of knowledge possessed by the נָבִיא or 'prophet' as compared with the כֹּהֵן or 'priest', it also seems worthy of note that the latter is never referred to as 'speaking' in Yahweh's 'Name', although, like king David (2 Sam. vi. 18 = 1 Chron. xvi. 2) or, indeed, the ordinary passer-by (Ps. cxxix. 8), he is described as pronouncing (*or* invoking) blessing in Yahweh's 'Name', i.e. Deut. x. 8, xxi. 5; 1 Chron. xxiii. 13.

[1] See above, pp. 4 ff.

[2] Cf. vii. 14: and, for a short discussion of the issues involved (with useful bibliographical references to date), see J. D. W. Watts, *Vision and Prophecy in Amos* (1958), pp. 9 ff.

[3] iii. 7.   [4] See above, p. 38, n. 5.   [5] xxiii. 21 f.: cf. 18.

And had declared My 'Words' to My people,
They would have turned them back from their evil way
And from their evil practices.

Thus Jeremiah shows by his own protests that these prophets whom he condemns elsewhere for their misleading
promises of 'Peace!'[1] were popularly regarded as indeed
standing in the inner Council of Yahweh and being made
acquainted with His secret purposes so that they might
act as His agents in fashioning the future; and the question inevitably arises as to what exactly was the status of
these professional intermediaries between Yahweh and His
people. Were they not, like the early prophets, actual cultic
officials? Should we not think of those in Jerusalem as being members of the Temple personnel in much the same
way as the priests?

Before we consider the evidence of the canonical prophets
themselves on this point, it is to be observed that the other
aspect of the prophetic function, i.e. that of calling upon (*or
with*) the 'Name' of Yahweh as compared with speaking
in His 'Name', is insufficiently recognized.[2] Nevertheless
the fact remains that, as the prophet was consulted with a
view to securing help and guidance from Yahweh, his role,
like that of the priest, was a dual one. He was not only

---

[1] See above, pp. 50 f.

[2] See, however, amongst the works cited above, p. 2, n. 1, Junker, pp. 36 f.,
von Rad, pp. 113 ff., Jepsen, pp. 200 f.; also J. Hempel, *Gott und Mensch im
Alten Testament*, B.W.A.N.T. 38, 2nd edit. rev. (1936), pp. 126 f., and, in
part, N. Johansson, *Parakletoi: Vorstellungen von Fürsprechern für die Men-
schen vor Gott in der alttestamentlichen Religion, im Spätjudentum und Ur-
christentum* (1940), pp. 3–21: and cf. now F. Hesse, *Die Fürbitte im Alten
Testament* (1949), pp. 39 ff.; A. S. Herbert, 'The Prophet as Intercessor',
B.Q. xiii (1949), pp. 76–80. For the expression קָרָא בְשֵׁם וגו׳, as used for the
invoking of Yahweh by a prophet, see above, pp. 54 f.; i.e. with reference to
1 Kings xviii. 24 and 2 Kings v. 11. Note, on the other hand, that there is
an element of ambiguity in the language of Ps. xcix. 6b, which, as normally
understood (cf. A.V., R.V., R.S.V.; and *Sacral Kingship in Ancient Israel*,
pp. 62 f.), would be apposite here: cf. the use of the expression קָרָא שֵׁם וגו׳ in
Deut. xxxii. 3, which suggests that in the former passage the Hebrew *may*
imply the 'proclaiming' rather than the 'invoking' of the divine Name, even
though at first sight the context seems to be against this.

the spokesman or messenger[1] of Yahweh; he was also the
representative of the people. Accordingly, just as the priest
became the specialist in sacrifice,[2] so the prophet was a
specialist in prayer; he was peculiarly qualified to act in
this way as an intercessor. A clear illustration of this fact is
already preserved in the E narrative of Genesis xx. Thus
Abimelech, king of Gerar, seeks intercourse with Sarah in
the belief that she is simply Abraham's sister, but through
the medium of a dream he receives timely warning against
carrying out his intention. The notable fact, however, is
that in the course of uttering his warning the divine visitor
says:[3]

Lo, thou art nigh to death on account of the woman whom thou
hast taken, for she hath a husband. . . . Now therefore restore the
man's wife, for, being a prophet, he may pray for thee; and so thou
mayest live.

Similar evidence is furnished by the canonical prophets.
Thus on one occasion (and this illustration is particularly
interesting in view of the above question as to whether or
not the Jerusalem prophets formed a part of the Temple
personnel) Jeremiah challenges his opponents to prove the
truth of their claim to be Yahweh's spokesmen, when they
affirm that the spoil already carried off from the Temple to
Babylon will soon be returned; and the proof is to consist
in their interceding successfully to prevent any more spoil
from finding its way from Jerusalem to Babylon, i.e.:[4]

If they be prophets and if the 'Word' of Yahweh be with them, let
them now entreat Yahweh of Hosts that the vessels which are left
in Yahweh's House and in the house of the king of Judah and in
Jerusalem may not go to Babylon.

[1] Cf. (i) the opening lines of the foregoing quotation from Jeremiah, and
(ii) the reference in Mal. ii. 7 to the priest as the 'Messenger' of Yahweh (as
above, p. 8).   [2] See above, pp. 3–9.   [3] Verses 3 and 7.
[4] xxvii. 18. As is clear from the context, the point is, not that the prophets
in question would already have made intercession along these lines if it had
been their function to do so (cf. Johansson, op. cit., pp. 20 f., in criticism of
von Rad, loc. cit.), but that, in Jeremiah's opinion, they were so obviously
out of touch with Yahweh that, if they were put to the test of making intercession along the lines indicated, they would be unable to exercise effectively
this aspect of the prophetic office which they claimed to hold.

Such passages[1] show quite clearly that, apart from possible practices of a magical or quasi-magical kind, the role of the prophet may be summed up under the dual aspect of (*a*) Prayer and (*b*) Oracle.[2] Of course, the foregoing emphasis upon the fact that the oracle might be sought must not be understood to suggest that it was given only on occasions of this kind. Nevertheless, the study of the canonical prophets in detachment from the general background of contemporary prophetic activity has meant that the oracular aspect of the prophetic function has been stressed—and perhaps, from a purely professional point of view, overstressed. As a result the intercessory aspect of the prophet's role has been more or less overlooked. Yet it is undoubtedly true that the נָבִיא or 'prophet', as a professional figure, was as much the representative of the people as the spokesman of Yahweh; it was part of his function to offer prayer as well as to give the divine response or oracle. This being the case, the question again arises as to what exactly was the status of these consultative specialists. Had they, like the early prophets, a standing within the cultus akin to that of the priests? In particular, should we think of the Jerusalem prophets as being members of the Temple personnel?

IV

An affirmative answer seems quite definitely demanded by the numerous passages, supplied for the most part by the canonical prophets themselves, in which, as in the example furnished by the cultus of the Tyrian Baal,[3] prophet and

---

[1] Cf. 1 Kings xiii. 6, xvii. 17 ff., xviii. 36 ff.; 2 Kings iv. 33, vi. 17 f. In keeping with what is said above, p. 2, n. 1, *ad fin.*, the cases in which a canonical prophet appears as such a specialist in prayer are reserved for separate treatment; but see, for example (in addition to the works cited above, p. 58, n. 2, and despite some reservations on the part of the present writer), the interesting and thought-provoking treatment of this subject by Hertzberg, *Prophet und Gott*, pp. 58 ff., 146 ff.

[2] See above, p. 22, n. 1, *ad fin.*

[3] See above, pp. 27 ff.

priest are found coupled together.[1] With a single exception[2] all these passages deal with the situation as it affects Jerusalem; so that here, in connexion with the Jerusalem Temple, one finds overwhelming proof of the fact that the prophets formed a vital[3] part of the cultic personnel. Thus on one occasion Jeremiah took his stand in the Temple court and threatened that, if the people failed to mend their ways, the sacred building would suffer a fate similar to that of the sanctuary at Shiloh, and the city itself would be laid waste.[4] His audience was apparently a large one, for the writer says:[5]

> The priests and the prophets and all the people heard Jeremiah speaking these words in the House of Yahweh.

As a result Jeremiah was brought before the magistrates and accused jointly by the priests and the prophets; but these failed to win the day. In short,[6]

> The magistrates and all the people said to the priests and the prophets: This man may not be sentenced to death, for it is in the Name of Yahweh our God that he hath spoken to us.

In the face of such a passage, coupled with all the preceding evidence, it is difficult to see how one can resist the conclusion that the prophets, quite as much as the priests, were officially connected with the Temple cultus. The same conclusion seems forced upon one when on another occasion Jeremiah is found making the following complaint:[7]

> Both prophet and priest are profane;
> Even in My House I have found their wickedness.
>   Oracle of Yahweh!

---

[1] See, in addition to the passages referred to in the text, Hos. iv. 4 f.; Isa. xxviii. 7; Jer. vi. 13, viii. 10, xiv. 18; Lam. iv. 13. Note, too, the significance which thus attached to such passages as Jer. iv. 9, viii. 1, xiii. 13; Mic. iii. 11; Zeph. iii. 3 f., despite the fact that in these cases priest and prophet are coupled together along with other representative members of society.

[2] Hos. iv. 4 f.

[3] Literally so: see above, pp. 49 f., and cf. *The Vitality of the Individual in the Thought of Ancient Israel*, pp. 88 ff.   [4] Jer. xxvi.

[5] Verse 7.   [6] Verse 16.   [7] Jer. xxiii. 11.

Indeed, there is some indication that, as might be expected, the prophets had special quarters (but not necessarily a permanent residence) within the Temple itself; for it is said that, when Jeremiah sought to put the Rechabites to the test, he took them into the Temple—[1]

to the room belonging to the 'sons' of Hanan ben Igdaliah, the 'man of God'.

The expression 'man of God', however, is a synonym for 'prophet'.[2] Accordingly, when one finds that the room in question apparently belongs to the 'sons' of a prophet, one can hardly do other than infer that the reference is to a particular school or guild of prophets forming part of the Temple personnel.[3] This being the case, it was doubtless in such circles that the various prophetic compositions were preserved.[4]

Thus there is abundant evidence from both the early and the late monarchical period to justify its being said of the prophets that, 'as in the case of the Baal cultus, they belonged in a certain sense, along with the priests, to the cultic personnel of the sanctuaries'.[5] In fact, as the evidence shows, one may go further and say that they belonged to the cultic personnel of the different sanctuaries in as real a sense as did the priests. Accordingly, one must beware of the added suggestion that they 'were there subject to the discipline of the superintendent priest'.[6] The illustrations offered in support of such a view, for example Jeremiah xxix. 26,[7] should be taken in quite a general sense. Thus the passage cited reveals the fact that there was a priest attached to the Jerusalem Temple whose duty it was to

---

[1] Jer. xxxv. 4.   [2] See above, p. 53, n. 1.   [3] See above, p. 17.

[4] See above, pp. 47 ff., and p. 22, n. 1, *ad fin.* It lies outside the scope of this work to deal with any such parallel amongst the canonical prophets as that which may be offered by the book of Isaiah (cf., for example, viii. 16), but the writer hopes to return to this point at a later date: cf. p. 2, n. 1, *ad fin.*

[5] Hölscher, *Die Profeten*, p. 143. Cf. the quotation from W. R. Smith, *The Prophets of Israel*, which is given above, p. 2, n. 1.

[6] Hölscher, loc. cit. Cf. Mowinckel, *Psalmenstudien III*, p. 17.

[7] Cf. Amos vii. 10 ff.; Jer. xx. 1 ff.

keep a check upon any wild behaviour; and, if one may
judge by what is known of religious festivals in the Near
East,¹ supervision of this kind was very necessary. It is
against such a background that one is able to see the exact
role of the official under discussion. It is not to be inferred
that he was there simply to put a check upon frenzied behaviour on the part of the prophets. In drawing such a
conclusion one is led astray by the use of the verbal form
הִתְנַבֵּא,² which is really employed here as a simple parallel to
שָׁגַע meaning 'to be frenzied, fanatic *or* mad' and, as in its
use with reference to Saul's malady,³ has no immediate connexion with prophets of any kind. This is made clear by the
fact that the official is said to be responsible for any individual (אִישׁ), not any prophet, who may act in this way.
Accordingly, when Amos and Jeremiah are respectively
subjected to the discipline of the superintendent priest at
Bethel and Jerusalem, it is for the quite general reason that
these outspoken (and, no doubt, from their opponents'
point of view fanatically outspoken) individuals are liable
to cause disturbance. This is important; for it is not to be
inferred that the prophets held a subordinate position in
the cultus. The fact is that (as one might have guessed
already from the relations existing between Nathan the
prophet and Zadok the priest in the early years of the
monarchy)⁴ their status was at least as high as, if not actually
higher than, that of the priests; for the latter not only co-
operated with them but, indeed, looked to them for guidance
in their administration. Once again it is Jeremiah who sheds
light upon the situation; for, speaking in the Name of Yahweh, he says:⁵

¹ Cf., for example, Lane, op. cit., pp. 464 ff.
² See above, pp. 17 f.
³ 1 Sam. xviii. 10: see above, p. 23.
⁴ See above, p. 27.
⁵ Jer. v. 30 f. For the rendering of עַל־יְדֵיהֶם, cf. Jer. xxxiii. 13; and esp.
1 Chron. xxv. 2, 3, and 6 (with reference to the musical guilds of the Jerusalem Temple as functioning 'under the direction of' their superiors): also
2 Chron. xxiii. 18, xxvi. 13; Ezra iii. 10. See also *The Vitality of the Individual
in the Thought of Ancient Israel*, p. 58, n. 1.

> An appalling and horrible thing
>   Hath happened in the land.
> The prophets prophesy falsely,
>   While the priests rule under their direction.
> As for My people, they love to have it so;
>   But what will ye do at the end thereof?

In view of the fact that the divine knowledge of the prophets was so essentially different from that of the priests in that it was derived from personal contact with Yahweh, such a position may be readily understood. In fact, one may say that it was almost inevitable. Fortunately Jeremiah supplies yet another illustration, throwing clear light upon the status of the prophets within the Jerusalem cultus, when he says:[1]

I also spoke to the priests and to all this people, saying: Thus saith Yahweh! Do not listen to the 'words' of your prophets who are prophesying to you, saying, 'The vessels belonging to the House of Yahweh will now soon be brought back from Babylon.' For it is a falsehood that they are prophesying to you.

Here the use of the possessive pronoun (i.e. *your* prophets) is sufficient to show that the prophets in question enjoyed official status; but, what is more, the fact that Jeremiah warns even the priests against paying any attention to their misleading promises must surely be held to indicate that it can hardly have been a very subordinate status.

All in all, therefore, the evidence for the cultic role of the prophets during the monarchical period, particularly so far as the Jerusalem Temple is concerned, may be regarded as sufficiently conclusive; and, this being the case, one can readily understand how it was that the poet who has left such a vivid picture of the final destruction of Jerusalem at the time of the Babylonian Exile could ask the anguished question:[2]

> Should there be slain in the sanctuary of the Lord
>   —priest and prophet?

Moreover, thus it is that at the time of the Restoration under Zerubbabel both prophet and priest are found to-

---

[1] Jer. xxvii. 16: cf. xxviii. 1 ff.   [2] Lam. ii. 20.

gether again and indeed (what is usually held to be remarkable) actually co-operating to rebuild the Temple;
for, whatever may have been the position with regard to
the earlier canonical prophets,[1] there can be no reasonable
doubt that Haggai and Zechariah, for example, were not
independent figures but members of a definite company
of prophets who had an official connexion with the cultus
and, in particular, showed a special responsibility for the
well-being of the Jerusalem Temple and its worship.[2] This
is borne out, for example, by the way in which Zechariah,
while seeking to encourage his hearers not to relax their
efforts in the long task of reconstruction, admits that in the
nature of the case they are still forced to hear[3]

the same words from the mouths of the prophets as were uttered at
the time when the foundation of the House of Yahweh of Hosts was
laid, namely, 'The Temple *must* be built'.

Even more instructive is the narrative which tells how a
deputation from Bethel (obviously representative of the
community as a social unit or 'corporate personality')[4] was
sent[5]

to entreat the favour of Yahweh, saying to the priests attached to the
House of Yahweh of Hosts and to the prophets, 'Am I to weep in the
fifth month, with fasting, as I have done these many years?'

Further, the answer to the inquiry is given by Zechariah,
who apparently acts as the spokesman of the other prophets;
for, while the reply is expanded and addressed directly to
the people at large and to the priests, the prophets are un-
mentioned.[6] Moreover, it may not be irrelevant to note that,
just as Haggai refers to the 'former' glory of the Temple,[7]
so Zechariah in giving the divine response appeals as on
other occasions[8] to the work of the 'former' prophets.[9]

---

[1] Cf. p. 2, n. 1, *ad fin.*
[2] Cf. Jepsen, op. cit., pp. 227 ff.
[3] Zech. viii. 9: cf. Ezra v. 1 f.
[4] See above, p. 50, n. 1.
[5] Zech. vii. 1 ff.
[6] Verse 5.
[7] ii. 3, 9.
[8] i. 4, vii. 12.
[9] Verse 7.

At this point, however, a question of fundamental importance is bound to arise; it becomes necessary to account for
the well-known disappearance of the prophetic function.[1]
Moreover, this disappearance may seem all the more remarkable, if it is thus true that at one time the prophet
enjoyed official status in close association with the Jerusalem
Temple and, indeed, continued to do so down to the time
of Nehemiah.[2] The explanation, however, appears to be
simple. In the first place, it seems probable that the Exile
brought the average type of professional prophet into considerable disrepute. Ezekiel, like Jeremiah, had sought to
warn his countrymen against the facile cheerfulness of those
prophets who

> prophesied unto Jerusalem and kept making for her an 'observation'
> of 'Peace!', when there was no peace.

Moreover, he had done so by likening the former to people
who build a wall and the latter to people who thereupon
coat it over with whitewash to hide its defects.[3] The final
fall of Jerusalem and the destruction of the Temple proved
him right, and brought disillusionment with regard to the
prophets who had lulled their hearers into fancied security

---

[1] For the type of 'prophet' condemned in Zech. xiii. 2–6, see above, p. 16,
n. 8.

[2] Cf. Neh. vi. 7, 10–14. The association of prophet and prophetess (נְבִיאָה)
in verse 14 raises the question as to how far the latter should be thought of as
enjoying the same cultic responsibilities as the former; and, despite the fact
that the remaining references to a prophetess in the Old Testament are so
few (i.e. Exod. xv. 20 (E); Judges iv. 4; 2 Kings xxii. 14; 2 Chron. xxxiv. 22;
Isa. viii. 3), two points of importance emerge in this connexion. Thus, in view
of the role attributed to Miriam, qua נְבִיאָה (Exod. xv. 20), in celebrating the
successful crossing of the Sea of Reeds (not to pursue further at this stage the
more debatable association of the so-called Song of Deborah with one who
is elsewhere described, like Miriam, as a נְבִיאָה, i.e. Judges iv. 4), it seems
clear that the prophetess had a leading part to play in connexion with
Israel's worship, and, this being the case, enjoyed a cultic role of some importance. Cf. Junker, *Prophet und Seher in Israel*, pp. 15 ff. Further, it seems
equally indicative of this importance *vis-à-vis* the cultus that, according to
2 Kings xxii. 11 ff. (2 Chron. xxxiv. 19 ff.), Josiah sent a deputation, including
the High Priest, to a prophetess, when he wished to obtain Yahweh's guidance in the disturbing matter of the law-book which had been found in the
Temple.

[3] See above, pp. 51 f.

by their reiterated promises of 'Peace!' This disillusionment appears, for example, in that poem which has already been mentioned as furnishing a vivid picture of this scene of destruction;[1] for the writer, addressing Jerusalem as a 'corporate personality', denounces these prophets in the following terms (and with apparent reference to Ezekiel's warning):[2]

> Thy prophets 'observed' for thee
> —nought but whitewash.[3]
> They did not reveal thine iniquity
> —to restore thy well-being.[4]

[1] See above, p. 64.   [2] Lam. ii. 14.

[3] *lit.* 'vanity and whitewash'. According to B.D.B. the Hebrew term תָּפֵל which occurs in the text is the adjective meaning 'tasteless', and is used figuratively of 'unsatisfying prophecies'. Cf. A.V. '(vain and) foolish things'; R.V. 'foolishness': see also K.B., s.v. The trouble, however, was that the messages in question were too satisfying (i.e. too much to the people's taste!); and it seems much more likely, therefore, that the writer intended the noun meaning 'whitewash', and had in mind a definite allusion to Ezekiel's warning picture. For the syntax of the clause as a whole, see Ezek. xiii. 6a as quoted above, p. 52 (with special reference to n. 3).

[4] The general significance of the expression which is rendered above by 'to restore thy well-being' seems now to be clearly established, even though its etymology may still be a matter of dispute. For a clear picture of the issues involved, see E. Preuschen, 'Die Bedeutung von שׁוּב שְׁבוּת im Alten Testamente', *Z.A.W.* xv (1895), pp. 1–74; L. Dietrich, שׁוּב שבות. *Die endzeitliche Wiederherstellung bei den Propheten*, B.Z.A.W. 40 (1925); E. Baumann, 'שׁוּב שבות. Eine exegetische Untersuchung', *Z.A.W.* xlvii (1929), pp. 17–44: also the admirably cautious summary of the views advanced in the foregoing works which is given by W. L. Holladay in his elaborate study, *The Root Šûbh in the Old Testament, with Particular Reference to its Usages in Covenantal Contexts* (1959), pp. 110 ff., although Holladay seems unduly sceptical when he argues that in Ps. lxxxv. 5 (EVV. 4) and Nahum ii. 3 (EVV. 2) we have no correspondingly clear examples of the *Qal* transitive use of √שׁוּב. For the rest, the present writer is inclined (*a*) to derive the form שְׁבוּת or שְׁבִית neither from √שׁבה ('to take captive') nor from √שׁוּב ('to return'), but from √*שׁבת ('to be firm') on the analogy of such forms as גְּמוּל and יְבוּל (?) *or* בְּרִיחַ and יְגִיעַ, and (*b*) to see the origin of this obviously technical expression in the ritual of the Sabbath (שַׁבָּת) as the day which was peculiarly qualified to give stability to the life of the community. Etymologically one may then compare the Arabic ثَبَتَ ('to be firm, stable') and such related nominal forms as ثُبُوت and ثَبَات ('firmness, stability, establishment *or* a state of being established'), bearing in mind also the striking fact that this Arabic root has come to be used of the Christian rite of 'Confirmation'. Cf. E. W. Lane, *An*

They 'observed' for thee oracles[1]
—that meant nought but exile.[2]

The promises of 'Peace!', though given in the Name of
Yahweh, had not been fulfilled;[3] and so, in accordance with
the test already laid down, apparently, by the D school,[4] these

Arabic–English Lexicon (1863–86); J. G. Hava, *Arabic–English Dictionary*,

rev. edit. (1915), s.v.: and, for the comparison of שְׁבוּת with ثَبُوت, Brockelmann, op. cit., § 143. However, the elaboration of this suggestion lies outside
the scope of the present monograph, and the writer must be content with the
hope that he may be able to return to it on another occasion.

[1] 'Oracles': i.e. plural of מַשְׂאֵת. Cf. מַשָּׂא, as above, p. 40, n. 4.

[2] *Or*, less probably, 'were nothing but misleading'. For the syntax of the
clause as a whole, see above, p. 67, n. 3, *ad fin.* (i.e. with reference to the
opening line).

[3] An utterance (√נשׂא) of this kind, which meant nought (שָׁוְא), involved a
breaking of the third commandment of the Decalogue: 'Thou shalt not utter
(√נשׂא) the Name of Yahweh thy God for nought (שָׁוְא).' Exod. xx. 7 (E);
Deut. v. 11. For the significance of √נשׂא, see above, p. 40, n. 4: and cf. S. R.
Driver, C.B. (1911), on the former passage; also Grether, *Name und Wort
Gottes im Alten Testament*, p. 21.

[4] The D school is alone in legislating for the prophet (Deut. xiii. 2–6
(EVV. 1–5), xviii. 9–22), and it is difficult to resist the impression that this
legislation also indicates disillusionment as to the reliability of the prophet;
for it is distinguished by a studied warning against the prophet whose 'word'
is not fulfilled (see above, pp. 51 ff.). It is not impossible, therefore, that this
Deuteronomic legislation concerning the prophet reflects the circumstances
of the Babylonian Exile. Indeed, one should, perhaps, bear in mind the
theory that the D school itself reveals an exilic point of view, which is
dominated by a consciousness of sin in that it regards the Exile as having
been brought about through infidelity to Yahweh. Cf. G. Hölscher, 'Kompo-
sition und Ursprung des Deuteronomiums', *Z.A.W.* xl (1922), pp. 161–255.
If this were so, the D school would offer further evidence of that sense of sin
and the accompanying disillusionment with regard to the prophets which
appear so clearly in Lam. ii. 14, as quoted above. On the other hand, of
course, if one may accept the more usual view that the D code, as such, had
its origin in Jerusalem during the seventh century, and especially if one be
prepared to emphasize a connexion with the north through an affinity with E
(cf. amongst the works cited above, p. 1, n. 1: Hempel, pp. 138 ff.; Oesterley
and Robinson, pp. 50 f.; Weiser, pp. 105 ff.; Anderson, pp. 38–45), or, if one
should see an origin in the north itself at about this time (cf. A. Alt, 'Die
Heimat des Deuteronomiums', in *Kleine Schriften zur Geschichte des Volkes
Israel*, ii (1953), pp. 250–75), it is possible that the apparent sense of disillusionment with regard to the prophets reflects the circumstances which
gave rise to an earlier exile—that occasioned by the deportations from the
Northern Kingdom in 733 and 721 B.C. Cf. Oesterley and Robinson, *A
History of Israel*, i, pp. 375 ff.; Noth, *Geschichte Israels*, pp. 234 ff., E.T.,
pp. 259 ff.; Bright, *A History of Israel*, pp. 255 ff.

prophets had been proved false. The disillusionment was obviously complete so far as many, if not all, of the prophets were concerned, although, as we have already observed, the author of this poem has so high a regard for the office itself as to contemplate with horror the thought that prophets should have shared with priests the fate of being slain in the very Temple itself.[1] Accordingly, if the feeling against the prophets could be expressed so forcibly at home, one is justified in supposing that it was even more intense in the exilic community itself. Indeed, there is reason to believe that, although these professional prophets were able to maintain their position for a time in the homeland, the reaction against them was so strong in Babylon that their loss of prestige ultimately found permanent expression in the work of the P school.

Thus in the work in question (taken as a whole) the cultic prophets appear as leaders of a number of choirs or, better perhaps, musical guilds, i.e. small but specific groups of individuals, combining the roles of both instrumentalists and singers, who enjoy special responsibility for the musical side of the Temple worship and thus obviously form a part of the Temple personnel; but now, being merged with the other Levitical orders, they are all in evident subjection to the (Aaronite) priesthood.[2] The revised account of Israelite history, which is to be found in 1 and 2 Chronicles, provides ample illustration of this fact; and, in turning to consider the evidence, it may be recalled that the first company of professional נְבִיאִים or prophets to be mentioned in the Old Testament are described as descending from a local sanctuary to the accompaniment of various musical instruments.[3] In the first place, then, there is the striking fact that in the

[1] See above, p. 64.

[2] Cf. Mowinckel, *Psalmenstudien III*, pp. 17 ff.; G. von Rad, *Das Geschichtsbild des chronistischen Werkes*, B.W.A.N.T. 54 (1930), pp. 113 f.; also Jepsen, op. cit., pp. 236 ff. As is indicated above, p. vi, a special acknowledgement is here due to Professor Otto Eissfeldt for his kindness in first drawing the writer's attention to this point and thereby encouraging him to proceed with this study.   [3] See above, p. 16.

account of David's arrangements for the conducting of the
Temple worship the verbal form נִבָּא, meaning 'to prophesy',
is used to sum up the duties of the individuals at the head
of a series of musical guilds or 'fraternities', who are described in the first place as the 'sons' of Asaph, the 'sons'
of Heman, and the 'sons' of Jeduthun;[1] and in the same
passage Heman, who is thus one of the three leading figures
under whose direction these musical guilds are to function,[2]
is described as 'the king's seer (חֹזֶה) in the "Words" of God
to lift up the horn'.[3] Similarly the other leading figures,

---

[1] 1 Chron. xxv. 1–6. See also on this remarkable passage Welch, *Prophet
and Priest in Old Israel*, p. 130, n. 2; *The Work of the Chronicler: its Purpose
and its Date* (1939), pp. 89 ff.; and Guillaume, op. cit., pp. 310 f. Reference
may also be made at this point to the account of the bringing up of the Ark
from the house of Obed-edom to the city of David, in 1 Chron. xv, where
(although the text is in some disorder and there is a measure of ambiguity)
the Levite Chenaniah is mentioned along with the singers in terms which
may imply that he had been appointed what one may call the 'oracle-master'
(verses 22 and 27). Cf. Mowinckel, loc. cit.; Pedersen, *Israel III–IV*, p. 117;
also J. Goettsberger, H.S.A.T. (1939), *in loc.*: but note the completely contrary view as represented by R. Kittel, H.K. (1902) and J. W. Rothstein,
H.S.A.T. (1923), who think that the primary reference must have been to
his responsibility for the actual 'carrying' of the Ark rather than the 'uttering'
of oracles. Cf. p. 40, n. 4, *ad fin.*, for the root under discussion; and see further, in recognition of the ambiguity in question, W. A. L. Elmslie, C.B.
(1899), I. Benzinger, K.H.C. (1901), M. Rehm, Echt.B., 2nd edit. rev.
(1956), H. Cazelles, S.B.J. (1954), W. Rudolph, H.A.T. (1955), *in loc.*, and
von Rad, op. cit., p. 110.

[2] See above, p. 63, n. 5.

[3] Verse 5. As is now generally recognized by commentators, the lifting up
of the horn is not to be understood as referring to the use of a musical instru-
ment (cf., for example, B.D.B., p. 927b, and the hesitant retention of this
view by Cazelles, op. cit., *in loc.*). It is a sign of success or well-being taken
from the animal world. Cf. (*a*) 1 Sam. ii. 10; Pss. lxxxix. 18 (EVV. 17) (K),
xcii. 11 (EVV. 10), cxlviii. 14; Lam. ii. 17; also Ps. lxxv. 5, 6 (EVV. 4, 5):
(*b*) 1 Sam. ii. 1; Pss. lxxv. 11 (EVV. 10), lxxxix. 18 (EVV. 17) (Q), 25 (EVV.
24), cxii. 9. Accordingly Heman's description agrees with what is known of
the Temple prophets. It was their function to create such success or well-
being; their 'words', as being the very 'Words' of Yahweh, were thought to
possess creative power. See above, pp. 36 ff., 49 ff. An example of such
prophetic 'lifting up of the horn', as affecting one of the kings of Judah, is
given below in the text, i.e. with reference to 2 Chron. xx. 1–30. It is now
usually held, of course, that the expression 'in the "Words" of God to lift up
the horn' should be construed closely with the latter part of the verse as
referring to the size of Heman's family and meaning 'in virtue of (*or* according to) the promise of God to lift up his horn (*or* exalt him)'. Cf. R.S.V.: and

Asaph and Jeduthun,[1] are each elsewhere described as a 'seer' (חֹזֶה);[2] and in this connexion it may be noted that, whereas in 2 Samuel xxiv. 11 Gad is called 'the prophet (נָבִיא), David's seer (חֹזֶה)', the former term is omitted in the corresponding passage in 1 Chronicles xxi. 9, and he is described simply as 'David's seer (חֹזֶה)'. A change of even greater significance, perhaps, is to be noted in the introduction to the story of Josiah's reform as contained in 2 Kings xxiii. 2 and 2 Chronicles xxxiv. 30. The former and earlier passage runs:

The king went up to the House of Yahweh and all the men of Judah and all the inhabitants of Jerusalem with him, the priests and the *prophets* and all the people both small and great.

The second and later passage, however, runs as follows:

The king went up to the House of Yahweh and all the men of

see further, for example, S. Oettli, K.K. (1889), Elmslie, op. cit., Benzinger, op. cit., Kittel, op. cit., E. L. Curtis and A. A. Madsen, I.C.C. (1910), Rothstein, op. cit., Goettsberger, op. cit., K. Galling, A.T.D. (1954), Rehm, op. cit., Rudolph, op. cit., and A. van den Born, B.O.T. (1960), each of whom follows this line. However, the fact that this interpretation tends to involve commentators in emending the text should be enough to make one pause before accepting, even in the emended form, so tortuous a way of expressing the thought in question. Moreover, the use of the idiom 'to lift up the horn' can only be described as a most unlikely way to express in *prose* the thought of God's bestowing any form of blessing: cf., for example, the language of 1 Chron. iv. 10, xi. 9, xiii. 14, xviii. 13, and esp. xxvi. 5; also 2 Chron. xxvi. 5. As is indicated above, the use of this idiom everywhere else in the Old Testament shows it to be characteristic, rather, of Israel's *psalmody*; and this fact is surely significant in the present connexion. If the usual view were correct, the use of the idiom in this prose passage would still call for comment, and it might then be held to support the theory that we have here a piece of prose narrative which comes from the circles of the musical guilds (cf., for example, Eissfeldt, *Einleitung in das Alte Testament*, pp. 665 ff.); but the present writer finds the view in question quite untenable. The fact that Heman is at least described as 'the king's seer' militates against the argument that the subject-matter of the context is that of a blessing bestowed upon Heman and not Heman's significance in relation to David (Rudolph, loc. cit.); and, what is more, in the corresponding contexts the cultic functions of both Asaph and Jeduthun are further defined and, indeed, in the case of Asaph defined with special reference to the king (cf. verses 2b and 3b), so that a corresponding further definition of the cultic role of Heman is not only in place but to be expected.

[1] Or Ethan: cf. 1 Chron. xv. 17, 19.

[2] 2 Chron. xxix. 30, xxxv. 15.

Judah and the inhabitants of Jerusalem, the priests and the *Levites* and all the people both great and small.

The alteration, as distinct, say, from the simple omissions and the final transposition, is of the first importance, for the term 'Levites' has been substituted for the term 'prophets'; and this may be held to confirm what is already suggested by the foregoing evidence, i.e. that the earlier prophetic guilds, such as that of the 'sons' of Hanan which formed a part of the Temple personnel in the time of Jeremiah,[1] have been converted into choirs or musical guilds and, as such, have been (*or* are being) merged with the other Levitical orders.[2]

Fortunately the preceding evidence is not all. The Chronicler actually gives a picture of a Temple prophet in the performance of his duty at a critical period in the reign of Jehoshaphat; but, in accordance with his point of view, he represents the prophet in question as a member, not of a prophetic guild, but of a Temple choir or musical guild— in short, as one of the 'sons' of Asaph.[3] The Moabites and Ammonites having invaded the Southern Kingdom and caused widespread alarm, a meeting representative of all the cities of Judah is held in the Temple with the express purpose of seeking Yahweh's aid. The king himself, acting as spokesman, prays for deliverance from the threatened danger; and the prayer is then followed by the divine response.

[1] See above, pp. 61 f.: and cf. 2 Chron. xxix. 25, as referred to above, pp. 15 f.

[2] The writer is aware, of course, that the Chronicler revises his sources to accord with his ideas of propriety, and that divergence between his accounts and the earlier sources must not be used uncritically. Cf. the foreign mercenaries of 2 Kings xi. 4–20 with the Levites of 2 Chron. xxiii; and see further, for example, Elmslie, Curtis and Madsen, Rudolph, op. cit., *in loc.* In the case of 2 Kings xxiii. 2 and 2 Chron. xxxiv. 30, however, the difference of terms does appear to have historical significance; for there is nothing in the Chronicler's general attitude to the pre-exilic prophets which might suggest that he varied the term 'prophets' here for any such reasons of propriety. It therefore seems likely that in this case he was modernizing the terminology so as to agree with the usage of his day.

[3] 2 Chron. xx. 1–30.

The way in which the latter is introduced, however, is remarkable; for the writer says:[1]

Then the Spirit of Yahweh came upon Jehaziel . . ., a Levite of the 'sons' of Asaph, in the midst of the assembly, and he said: 'Pay heed, all Judah, and ye inhabitants of Jerusalem, and thou king Jehoshaphat! Thus saith Yahweh to you . . . .'

The answer to Jehoshaphat's prayer very significantly proves to be a promise of 'victory' (יְשׁוּעָה),[2] a typical oracle of 'Peace!'; and it is therefore highly interesting to find that, as the people go out against the enemy, Jehoshaphat exhorts them in the following terms:[3]

Maintain faith in Yahweh your God, that ye may be maintained![4]
Maintain faith in His prophets, and thus meet with success!

Finally, to complete the picture, 'victory' is secured, not by any military prowess on the part of Jehoshaphat and his forces, but through the strategy of Yahweh Himself.[5] Thus there is no escaping the fact that the narrative under discussion presents an embellished picture of what has been shown to be one of the duties of the prophets, the ensuring of success in time of war; and it is not without significance that it is Jehoshaphat who figures in two of the most striking illustrations of this aspect of the prophetic function—those contained in the earlier records of 1 Kings xxii and 2 Kings iii.[6] Indeed, it may well be that in the actual incident on which this narrative is probably based the oracle was given by a Temple prophet following some such musical stimulation as that which is linked with the oracular activity of

---

[1] Verses 14 f.   [2] Verse 17: cf. p. 40, n. 1.   [3] Verse 20.

[4] Note the word-play by means of the *Hiph'îl* and *Niph'al* of √אמן. The similar word-play in Isa. vii. 9 occurs readily to mind; but this must be reserved for separate treatment under consideration of the role of the canonical prophets and their relation to the cultus.

[5] See above, pp. 36 ff.; but the further implications of this point must also be reserved for separate treatment. Meantime, cf. A. Bentzen, 'Quelques remarques sur le mouvement messianique parmi les juifs aux environs de l'an 520 avant Jésus-Christ', *R.H.P.R.* x (1930), pp. 493–503, esp. 499 ff.; Hempel, *Gott und Mensch im Alten Testament*, pp. 108 ff., *Das Ethos des Alten Testaments*, pp. 96 ff.   [6] See above, pp. 19 f.

Elisha in the latter passage.[1] Be that as it may, the narrative as a whole offers final proof of the fact that under the influence of the P school the prophet has been made completely subordinate to the priest. Indeed the prophet, as a member of the Temple personnel, is no more; his place has been taken by the Temple singer.

Thus, to sum up, there is considerable evidence both in the more definitely historical records of the Old Testament and in the messages of the canonical prophets themselves to show that during the monarchy (and, in a measure, for some two centuries later) the נָבִיא, *qua* professional 'prophet', was an important figure in the personnel of the cultus—

---

[1] De Vaux, *Les Institutions de l'Ancien Testament*, ii, p. 251, appears to think that the force of the passage under discussion is nullified and the case for the existence of cultic prophets thereby undermined because, on his interpretation of 2 Chron. xxiv. 20, Zechariah, the son of Jehoiada the priest, is there described as undergoing possession by the divine 'Spirit' while in the Temple and thereupon rebuking his contemporaries in prophetic terms, although there is no evidence to show that Zechariah was a member of a Temple choir or musical guild such as that which is described in action above. In reply to this, however, it must be pointed out in the first place that the language of the verse is so summary that, far from referring to a single incident involving a sudden accession of the 'Spirit' analogous to that which is described in 2 Chron. xx. 1–30, it seems to carry the broader implication that Zechariah was inspired or, rather, emboldened (cf. the corresponding use of √לבשׁ in Judges vi. 34; also 1 Chron. xii. 19 (EVV. 18)) to make a public stand on Yahweh's behalf against his fellow countrymen over what may well have been a period of time, for we learn in the following verse that he ultimately suffered martyrdom in the Temple precincts as the result of a conspiracy which had secured the support of the king. The second and more important point to be made, however, is that, even if de Vaux were right in his interpretation of this passage, it would still be valueless as evidence against the existence of cultic prophets; it would merely serve to show that we must allow for the existence of a 'free' or 'charismatic' type of prophecy, and, as is pointed out above, p. 22, n. 3, the present writer has been careful to envisage this possibility from the first. In other words, the passage cited by de Vaux belongs, at most, to the additional data which will need to be taken into account when considering the relationship of the canonical prophets to the cultus; and that is a problem which, in the present writer's opinion, cannot be dealt with satisfactorily until due consideration has also been given to the evidence available (but unfortunately so long neglected) for the existence of something other than this 'free' or 'charismatic' type of prophecy. In short, the argument advanced by de Vaux offers merely another example of that over-simplification of the issues against which the present writer has already had occasion to protest.

particularly that of the Jerusalem Temple. As such, his function was to promote the שָׁלוֹם or 'welfare' of the people, whether that of the individual or that of society at large. To this end his role was a dual one. He was not only the spokesman of Yahweh; he was also the representative of the people. He was not only a giver of oracles; he was also expert in the technique of addressing Yahweh, i.e. in the offering of prayer. The disaster of the Babylonian Exile, however, involved the cultic prophet in a certain loss of prestige; and, although he was able to maintain his position for a time in the homeland, the reaction against him was so strong in Babylon that this loss of prestige ultimately found permanent expression in the work of the P school, which reduced him to the rank of an ordinary Temple singer. In this way, being merged with the other Levitical orders, he was brought into definite subjection to the priesthood—and so disappeared.[1]

---

[1] This is not to be taken as necessarily the whole of the story; but a fuller picture cannot be given until we have solved the problem as to just how the canonical prophets are to be seen, individually, against this general background (or perhaps, in some cases, within this setting) of cultic prophecy.

INDEX

(a) SUBJECTS

Where relevant page numbers apply to both text and footnotes.

INDEX

(b) AUTHORS

Page numbers refer throughout to the footnotes.

INDEX

(c) SCRIPTURE REFERENCES

Where relevant page numbers apply to both text and footnotes.
All references are to the Hebrew text.

INDEX

(d) SELECT HEBREW WORDS AND PHRASES

Where relevant page numbers apply to both text and footnotes.

PRINTED IN GREAT BRITAIN
AT THE UNIVERSITY PRESS, OXFORD
BY VIVIAN RIDLER
PRINTER TO THE UNIVERSITY